The Praise of 'Sons of Bitches'

"Man is a social animal or son of a bitch, as God and the prophets warned since the beginning."

Arthur Miller, "When Time had at least a Form," *The New York Times*, Jan. 24, 1971

The Praise of 'Sons of Bitches'
On the Worship of God by Fallen Men

James V. Schall

St. Augustine's Press
South Bend, Indiana

Manufactured in the United States of America.

1 2 3 4 5 6   25 24 23 22 21 20 19

Library of Congress Cataloging in Publication Data
Schall, James V.
The praise of 'sons of bitches' : on the worship of God by fallen men
/ James V. Schall. – 2nd edition.
pages cm
1. Worship. 2. Christian life – Catholic authors. I. Title.
BV10.3.S33 2015
264 – dc23   2015005688

∞ The paper used in this publication meets the minimum requirements of the American National Standard for Information Sciences - Permanence of Paper for Printed Materials, ANSI Z39.48-1984.

St. Augustine's Press
www.staugustine.net

CONTENTS

The following chapters have appeared in other form in the following places.

Chapter I: University Bookman, Spring, 1972, New York.

Chapter II: Catholic World, March, 1971, New York.

Chapter III: Vital Speeches, 15 November 1976, New York.

Chapter IV: Review for Religious, November, 1974, St. Louis, Missouri.

Chapter V: Not previously published.

Chapter VI: The Way, Supplement, Summer, 1977, London.

Chapter VII: Doctrine and Life, Supplement, V. 13, n. 60, 1975, Dublin.

Chapter VIII: To be published by Spiritual Life, Washington, DC.

Chapter IX: Catholic World, August, 1971.

Chapter X: Catholic World, November, 1970.

Chapter XI: To be published by The Catholic Digest, St. Paul, Minnesota.

Chapter XII: The Commonweal, 8 April, 1972, New York.

Chapter XIII: To be published in Worship, Collegeville, Minnesota.

Chapter XIV: University Bookman, Autumn, 1974, New York.

Introduction to the American Edition

"The plaque outside the door at Casamari reads: SI-LENTIUM. The word, 'solitary,' is not to be applied to God. There is nothing in all creation so like God as stillness."

From Chapter VII, "On Loneliness and Silence."

"'Only God can make a safe toy. . . .' I wonder if Mr. Glass (a toy designer who spoke these words to the Chicago City Council in 1972) knew that the aging Plato . . . in his *Laws*, called men the 'playthings' of God? I hope that he didn't, in a way. For these curious human toys that God did make are anything but 'safe.' That is, in fact, why God made them. For had the Deity made men 'safe.' creatures with no real sense of doom, there would have been no sense in making them in the first place. *Because we are not safe, we are.*'"

–From Chapter XIV, "On God's Jokes, Toys, and Christmas Trees."

I.

This oddly-titled, but theologically resonant, book was written largely during the years from 1969–1977 when I was teaching one

1

semester at the Gregorian University in the center of Rome and the other semester at the University of San Francisco, just beyond the edge of Golden Gate Park. In the Spring of 1978, I began teaching full time at Georgetown University in Washington, just above the Potomac River, where I remained until my retirement, in 2012, to Los Gatos in the Santa Cruz Mountains of California. This book has long been a favorite of mine. I am pleased that there now is an American edition of it, thanks to Bruce Fingerhut and St. Augustine's Press. This book retains a few mostly forgotten names like Idi Amin. Its content, I think, remains fresh and alert to ultimate things seen in the context of this world, which all of us inhabit for a few years in order to decide in our freedom how we shall live the eternal life offered to us.

Three books that I have always, in retrospect, conceived to be "companions," or perhaps offsprings, of this book are my *Unexpected Meditations Late in the XXth Century* (Franciscan Herald 1985), *Idylls & Rambles: Lighter Christian Essays* (Ignatius Press 1994), and *On the Unseriousness of Human Affairs* (ISI Books 2001). St. Augustine's Press published *Remembering Belloc* (2013) and *The Classical Moment: Selected Essays on Knowing and Its Pleasures* (2014), both of which, as does this book, fall in the general sphere of my wonderment about existing things, things that need not exist, but do.

The Praise of "Sons of Bitches" I have always called my "English" book. It was originally published in 1978 by St. Paul Publications, which had the wonderful address of "Middlegreen," Slough, in Berkshire. We often, in the days before Amazon's mailings, laughed at the title. We envisioned that potential purchasers of a more delicate make-up might feel that it was wiser to carry the book, with its title, from the shop in a paper bag. The title is intended to be amusing, though it is provocative. It bears a meaning, when sorted out, that gets to the heart of things.

But the subtitle, in a sense, carries the weight of the book — *"On the Worship of God by Fallen Men."* This sub-title was used in the days when one did not have to explain grammatically why

2

the abstract word "man" included both males and females. And it is a book about praise and what is worthy of it. Contrary to what we might expect, it is not the perfect that most need to worship God, but the imperfect, the fallen, those who have the most distance to go, more to make up. In other words, just because we are fallen, it does not mean that we are forgotten. This too is what redemption is about.

The whole title, as I indicate on the page just before the title page, came from a short comment of the playwright, Arthur Miller, in 1971. In a memorable passage, he remarked that we are all *either* "social animals" *or* "Sons of Bitches," as God and the Prophets have "warned" from the beginning. My addendum to this remarkable observation and, hence, the theme of the book is that we are not either/or, but both/and. That is, we are all fallen and all redeemed. But this double condition means, as I imply in the citation to begin this Introduction, that we are "risks" of God in our very being. He could not create us to be "determined" and still fashion us to be what we are, namely, free beings. Nor could He redeem us without our input, our acceptance. Thus, those who properly "worship" God are, in fact, both fallen and redeemed. They are neither pure spirits nor inhabitants of an original state of justice that knew no fall, no sin.

The phrase "Sons of Bitches" is, I suppose, a very masculine one that grows out of the comradery of good men — "Joe, you old 'sonofabitch,' it is good to see you again." In context, the phrase has a certain earthy affection to it, a certain familiarity with our fallenness and with our glory, even with our kinship with the animals. That, at least, is the spirit of the title, which, I hope, like all good titles, draws our curiosity and attention to a truth we need to live by, to a truth we never quite put in proper order to see what it means. We find, then, a certain whimsicalness in these chapters. The four sub-sections are entitled, respectively: "Who We Are," "How We Fail," "What Saves Us," and "What We Do When All Else Is Done."

The chapters in this book originally appeared as essays in various journals. When someone sets out to write, contrary to what we might suppose, he never quite knows where it will lead and end. Often things that were written independently, on reflection, go together. That is the feeling that I had with regard to the chapters in this book. When assembled, they did seem to belong together. On the surface, it is but a collection of disparate essays on various topics. And in fact, I happen to love collections of sundry essays even if they do not seem to go together. But they can also, as I hope they do here, fall into intelligible and related categories and themes. They can broaden and deepen what went before. They can point to where we are going while yet retaining their own inner coherence. Many of the themes and sentences here reverberate through my mind with an almost enchanting resonance — "the stillness," "*because we are not safe, we are.*"

II.

As I look over this book some thirty-five years after its publication, I am reminded of many people, scenes, and musings that I had almost forgotten, but which I remember well when reading of them again. As this was originally an "English book," I find things "English" in it. In the *St. Austin Review* for a number of years, I did a series of columns I called: "English Essays." I seldom write anything in which Samuel Johnson, Chesterton, C. S. Lewis, Tolkien, or Belloc do not appear somehow. In one sense, I can almost say that Belloc taught me to walk, or at least to see what is there when I do walk. In my *Sum Total of Human Happiness* (St. Augustine's Press, 2006), the first Chapter is entitled: "*The Path to Rome*: Belloc's (1901) Walk after a Century: On Being 'Reasonably' Happy in This Life," while the last Chapter is entitled: "Belloc's Second Walk, a Century Later (*The Four Men*) (1902): On the Character of Enduring Things." The phrases, "being reasonably happy in this world" and "enduring things," both haunt me and please me.

So in the first chapter of this book, I laughed to myself when I recalled once having purchased on Gary Street in San Francisco a copy of the legendary English satirical journal, *Punch*. It was once edited by Malcolm Muggeridge, another amazing Englishman. Therein I found an article explaining that the trouble with the English was that they were too polite to get anything done. They were not like the Yankees who complain about everything and hence worked wonders. You get ahead in the world by telling everyone how bad things are. So the advice that the article offered to the English was this: "Given a choice between two evils: 'CHOOSE BOTH! *Find a little bad in the best of things.*'" In its own way, if we think about it, that admonition is but another way to speak about "the worship of God by fallen men," about the "praise of Sons of Bitches." One can only laugh at the wit and the wisdom shown in this classic advice to Englishmen about how, like the Yankees, to get things done when it is your politeness that holds you back.

I was present at the first public Mass celebrated in San Francisco's new cathedral in October 1970. As I had been in England and Europe, the reality of great cathedrals was on my mind at the time. This contest was the occasion of the second chapter on building cathedrals and tearing them down. This new Nervi Cathedral, St. Mary's, at Turk and Gough Streets, struck me as a most beautiful structure, one worthy of the ages.

So I went back and reflected on the cathedrals that I had previously seen, many of the great ones. I also recalled Samuel Johnson's trip to the Hebrides and his stop at St. Andrew's in Scotland, a great cathedral that had been, evidently for theological reasons, ravished in the Reformation. Also there were always those, and San Francisco was no exception, who thought that the money spent on cathedrals would be better spent on the poor. This view always seemed wrong-headed to me.

From this experience of cathedrals, one of my favorite themes has been that the "poor need beauty even more than bread." In fact, to offer the poor bread but not beauty is a high point in dehumanization. The poor man in Europe owned the cathedrals as much as the rich. Cathedrals were often built over centuries by small towns. To deprive a people of beauty was a form of barbarism. And this was not to mention the theme of Henry Adams that it was precisely the cathedrals that were the dynamos of growth. But this enterprise was caused by the Virgin, by the worship of God that came out of the abundance of things. The real issue was not beauty or bread, but both. The spirit that could erect the cathedrals was much more likely also to know how to bake bread.

The chapter on sincerity (IV) I have always thought to be of particular relevance, even more so today than when it was first written. Sincerity can indeed be called a virtue, but it is not one of the classical virtues. We have largely come to judge men not on what they do or on the truth but on the "sincerity" with which they do it. Even the Supreme Court in the Hobby Lobby cases seems to have embraced this view.

The "insincere" man is the one who does not really believe or hold what he says or does. There is something of a biblical Pharisee here. But simply because a man is "sincere" about what he does or says tells us nothing about the truth or validity of his ideas. In fact, the most dangerous men are often quite sincere in what they maintain. Thus, I considered "sincerity" to be the most "dangerous" virtue. It prescinded from the necessary discussion of what one is sincere about. A good part of the classical moral order has been overturned because its corrupters were "sincere" in holding dangerous and harmful positions. While there is something most attractive in a "sincere" man who believes what he holds, still there can be something most unsettling about him when his sincere beliefs are taken seriously.

The love of animals, though usually in its own way sincere, has become increasingly a topic as the relative difference between animals and men are often obscured (Chapter III). Not a few who write on the demographic decline obvious in much of the world note that dogs and other animals replace babies as the concern of people. No doubt, there is a proper relation of men and animals. Scripture talks of the good shepherd and St. Francis is the patron of animal lovers. There was a time when hunting and fishing were a necessary part of a family's well-being. But today, most animals are pets. Horses are not work but recreation animals. Those animals that are used for food are grown in massive concentrations and not around the farm with other animals, as I recall from my Iowa boyhood.

Probably it is best not to use the word "love" of animals. Something like "affection" is more appropriate. Animals are good beings in their own order. But they are not rational. When taken out of nature, where they depend on their own instincts for survival and continuation in the species, they become dependent directly on man. Hence we have the veterinary industry, the huge business of dog and cat food, and all the other things that have to do with domesticated animals.

I myself have never been much of a fan of having animals around a home, but I know too many families or people whose pet is an important part of their life. The place of animals among human things is, like other virtues, something that can be a too much or a too little. When animals become more important than human beings in our lives, something is wrong. But a world bereft of animals would surely be a lonely one. Animals are the mediators between the plants and the humans on this planet. They all have a proper place, and an improper one.

While the love of animals is a relatively easy concern to deal with, the love of enemies is rather more difficult (Chapter VIII). The admonition to love one's enemy is both startling and difficult to deal with. Obviously, the love of enemies does not mean capitulation to whoever threatens us. The way Lincoln admonished us — "with malice towards none and with charity to all"

— to deal with the defeated South in his Second Inaugural Address is a classic example of a proper love of enemy. In the ancient world, defeated enemies were simply wiped out. The love of enemies includes the restoration of order to their lives. And there is the question of who is just and who is unjust. The love of enemies was not designed to suggest that nobody had any enemies. While the New Testament tells us to love our enemies, it is full of warnings about enemies who hate us.

An "enemy" can be someone whose deeds and words are truly disordered and hateful, but the good man is often an enemy of the wicked one. We take it for granted that a wicked man does not love his enemies. We also do not want love of enemy to condone the enemy's wrongdoing. The love of enemies and the turning the other cheek were in part designed to cause change and repentance in the enemy. When we love our enemy, we are not asked to love their wickedness, nor are we asked to capitulate before evil as if we were not responsible for doing what we could about it.

III.

The chapters on "loneliness and silence" and on "sadness and laughter" have been favorites of mine (Chapters VII and IX). Every Holy Saturday, somehow, I think of the theme of "stillness" which is found in the chapter on loneliness and silence. When the Lord is in the tomb on Holy Saturday, an ancient hymn imagined that the whole world was in "stillness." Though we are beings who are born to live in society among others, something incomplete hovers about us even in society.

Chesterton talked about "being homesick at home." But home is the last place in which we should be "homesick," of course. Yet, we will never find in this life that for which we are created. This emptiness is why the doctrine of the Trinity floats through the pages of this book. The inner life of the Godhead is our real end. We will always have a certain loneliness in our hearts in this world, a healthy one that reminds us that nothing we find or encounter is really our final home.

I have never forgotten the theme found in the chapter on sadness and laughter (IX). Most good comedians, I read somewhere, were often sad in their personal lives. When I was younger, I had a theme in my head that I could not get rid of — "Would you abolish sadness, if you could?" Even though we are created for eternal life, we would not abolish the sadness of this life. To do so would be to eliminate the consequences of our acts. Sadness is a sign that reminds us of our fallenness, but also the hope of laughter.

The very existence of laughter is one of the great mysteries of our existence. There are many kinds of laughter, of course, even a diabolical kind, that we shudder to hear. But genuine laughter is difficult both to define and to explain. Yet, we know that it is fundamental to our being. Somehow it makes everything lighten up, seem worthwhile. Moreover, joy and laughter are really more difficult to explain than sadness and even evil.

We are finite beings surrounded by sadness, yet we laugh. We see that sadness is not the purpose of our existence even though it belongs to it, to the kind of existence we have been given, the only kind there is for us. Such thoughts always bring me to the last words of Chesterton's *Orthodoxy*, a book I dearly love. And there he said that the only thing that Christ did not show us in his stay among us was his "mirth." It was not because he had none, of course, but because he had so much of it. If we saw it, we could not bear it. The divine gladness is, for now, more than we could bear but not more than we are promised.

The chapter on "playing" brings up a theme that has long interested me (Chapter X). If I said that this chapter is about sports, it would be true. But what I found over the years was that it is sports that, when sorted out, can help lead us to understand the highest things. Many complain that sports are a kind of bread and circuses, or a waste of time. And paradoxically they are a "waste of time," but in that sense of the *Little*

Prince. He told us that only the time that we "waste" with our friends is worth much.

Aristotle is the one who alerted me here, but Plato made the whole issue transcendent. Aristotle said that watching games was near to contemplation, though not so serious a subject matter. Out of this remark, I have always observed the puzzlement in young men in particular but also young women in their desire to explain why they like to watch sporting contests. They suspect something more basic is at issue but are told that it is mostly frivolous.

Mostly, they are told that the experience of watching a good game does not press deeply in the human soul. I tend to think, however, that this riveting experience is the first lesson in what it means to behold things "for their own sakes." This beholding is the real contemplative mood. Most of us learn what it means when we suddenly find ourselves, as it were, outside of ourselves, locked into the ongoing play of a good game.

But it was only when I came to the passage in Plato that told us that human affairs are not very "serious" that I really understood. He called us the "playthings of God.", hat is, we need not exist but did. This theme will lead me in this book to the last chapter, probably of all the essays I have written, my favorite. It is not that Plato thought human affairs had no point. But compared to what was really "serious," namely, the things of God, they were not so important. The beholding that takes us out of ourselves in games is but a mere hint of the beholding for which we are created and in which we find our happiness.

Since the "worship" of God by fallen men is the very context of this book, I have two chapters on worship, one on the Breviary, or Divine Office, and one on what "worship" itself might be about (Chapter XIII). I have come to realize that the proper worship of God cannot be a totally humanly formed effort. In the eons before and after revelation in Christ, there were many forms of rite that attempted to show some praise of God. Sometimes it was the sacrifice of a bull or calf, other times of grain, rarely, but perversely, even of human sacrifice. The coming of Christianity put something new in the universe. This new reality was that God taught us the proper way to worship Him.

This proper way is what the sacrifice of the Mass is about. There is to be present in the world from the rising of the sun to its setting a "perfect praise" in the world. This perfect praise is what the Mass is. The Church is not so much a human institution to tell us how to do human things, but a society made up of dying individuals who are instructed in divine things. The virtue of "religion" is the philosophical response that men make to God for His reality. But for Christians, worship contains the instruction of God about how to worship Him. This is what was shown at the Last Supper. The proper way to worship God is made known to us by God.

IV.

In Christianity there is not only a place for play, justice, and worship, but also a place for truth (Chapter XII). In his "Regensburg Lecture," Pope Benedict sketched out the need that civilizations have within them for universities. Universities arose in the Christian West as a response largely to the introduction of Aristotle into its midst. The question was: "How did Aristotle know so much without the benefits of revelation?" This concern led to the idea, already reflected in Plato's Academy and Aristotle's Lyceum, of an institution within society, yet apart from it, that would be free of outside pressure so that it could examine the truth of things without fear of reprisal. The Church, the monastery, the city, and the university each had its proper place within the civilization. All of these institutions, in turn, depended on truth. A university had to have a certain freedom from outside pressures for it to be what it was intended to be, a place for the disciplined pursuit of truth. The question arose, then, about the relation to the knowledge from and in revelation to the knowledge that could be figured out by reason, the model of which was Aristotle.

Christianity did not conceive revelation to be based on subjective feeling or sentiment, but on a truth that was rooted in objective reality. The truth found in revelation, in turn, was addressed to the truth of reason, of *logos*. And truth was not rooted in the methods to find it. Philosophy, and thus the university, was to be open to all truth not just that limited to certain methods. The monastery, moreover, was the original place where these searchings after truth were unified and directed to both the worship of God and to the service of man. What revelation added to reason, besides certain answers to its own questions, was the idea that truth, virtue, and salvation were not directed only to a certain elite, but to all men. This was the heritage that formed the West and the universalism of the truths and rites that were directed to all men in their particularity.

The final chapter in this book actually arises from the notion of Christmas — its mood, its joy, its symbols, and its gifts. Christmas is largely driven out of the public eye today. We are lessened by it, all of us. Its reason for existing is turned into a winter festival and a series of meaningless abstractions. Josef Pieper had often said that all real joy and celebration arise from worship, from having something worthwhile being joyful about. Within Christianity, we can find two ways to approach the idea of gift. But first, we must recognize that our very lives are gifts, as is the world itself. Its character, as is that of our individual lives, is that of having been first given to us.

"Nothing that you do not give away will ever be truly yours," or so I recall reading somewhere. Malcolm Muggeridge tells us, along with St. Paul, that the real joy is in the giving. Aristotle pictures the magnanimous man as one who gives of his abundance to others. Yet, I once was in a class in graduate school with a famous Viennese professor, Rudolf Allers. He remarked one evening in class that while it might be more "blessed" to give than to receive, still it was more difficult to receive. We are praised for giving. We can only be thankful for receiving. Our receiving something is a classic sign of our self-insufficiency. That has become the theme of this last chapter and indeed, I hope the theme of this book. "The joy is in the receiving." Giving is fine, but receiving is a better sign of our understanding of ourselves as fallen men, as, yes, "Sons of Bitches" who exist first by virtue of someone else's gift. In the end, we receive our final invitation to complete our lives not from ourselves but as a *donum Dei*, as a gift of God. It is not something we made from our own imagination. It was Thomas More who advised us, as we see in the Conclusion, to "lead our lives calmly and cheerfully." When "fallen men" worship God, surely this is what they are doing — leading their lives calmly and cheerfully. The gift, they know, comes in the receiving.

James V. Schall, S.J.
Professor Emeritus, Georgetown University
Los Gatos, California
Feast of St. Bonaventure, 2014.

Part I

WHO WE ARE

Chapter I

ON MEN IN SEARCH OF GLORY

Once in a rare while, we come across a sentence or a phrase that keeps ringing in our memory, ringing perhaps because it sounds at least partly true, mostly because of the very sound itself. Two lines keep coming back to me. I am not, indeed, fully sure what they mean, yet they strike me somehow as being of more than ordinary importance. Perhaps by writing them down, I can understand them or forget them. The first I once found in an essay about the Chairman of an Italian Parliamentary Commission then charged with investigating the Mafia.[1] The writer, Egidio Sterpa, worried to himself whether the frequent accusations were true that that particular minister, whom Sterpa called "The Sherlock Holmes of the Anti-Mafia", was merely seeking his own political advancement.

On second thought, however, Sterpa questioned his own premise. Is such concern for political advancement really so bad, after all? Even more fundamentally, "La democrazia ha bisogno di gente alla ricerca di gloria . . .". That is the sentence I cannot forget — "Democracy has need of men in search of glory". There are needs and realities beyond the ordinary, beyond even political ambitioning, usefulness, and reward that men also search for. There are simply some values beyond politics. "Glory", to be sure, is both a divine attribute — *Soli Deo Gloria* (Glory to God

17

Alone), Luther said — and a Machiavellian one — *Soli Principi Gloria* (Glory to the Prince Alone). The *Doxa*, the *Gloria*, the Glory is the concentration, as it were, of something's goodness and beauty merely for its own splendour. What it already is, is that for which all else is. To limit the requirements of society and man merely to motives of greed or reward or self-interest is to imprison, to cripple.

The second phrase I cannot quite forget was in *La Stampa*, written in connection with the thesis of the now famous young Soviet critic, Andrej Amalrik, the one since exiled from Russia, who questioned whether there would even by a Soviet Union by 1984. Nicola Chiaromonte brooded about this unexpected argument of Amalrik because he feared the same disease that was sapping the spiritual strength of Russia was also at an advanced stage in the West. "Can we really say", Chiaromonte asked, "that in our lands the thought of the majority is much elevated above that of the 'manual level' (as in Russia)? We have certainly a 'mechanized' level and even a 'televised' level. But is that so superior to the manual?" Then he added — and this was the sentence that bothered me — "Today, man's greatest enemy is optimism".[2] This optimism is evil because it causes our consciences to sleep, and this merely worsens the destructive forces already at work in our society.

When in England . . .

This, of course, is rather a sombre outlook. The English put it better. One autumn I remember buying the last copy of *Punch* in a bookshop on Geary Street in San Francisco. The trouble with the English, it chided, was that they were too polite. The reason they never got ahead in this world was because they did not, like the Yankees, complain and bitch about everything. Only those groups that gripe, that insist on how badly off they are, ever get ahead in this cruel world. "Given a choice between two evils", the

18

English were advised by this impeccable source, "CHOOSE BOTH! *Find a little bad in the best of things . . . !"*

W. C. Fields used to think this was the main English problem also. Robert Lewis Taylor wrote of him: "The lopsided romance between Fields and the English continued off and on for years. On subsequent tours, at each unusual expression of their good manners, he worked out some compensating mischief".[3] Apparently, Fields even developed his philosophy of "Never give a sucker an even break" from his experience with the English. He seemed to have gained his basic insight from watching an American confidence man by the name of "Doc" Atterbury operate in this instance:

> In Fields' presence, Atterbury had taken a seat on a train and lit a cigar, in violation of the rules, as stated clearly in every car. A stranger on the opposite seat demurred, pointing to the sign. Gazing serenely out of the window, Atterbury continued to smoke, pausing only to flick off his ash. The stranger became increasingly upset and argumentative. At length he pulled out a card and cried, "Perhaps you don't know who I am, sir?" Atterbury's scrutiny of the landscape was undisturbed, but the complainant succeeded in forcing the card between two of his fingers, after which Atterbury put the card in his vest pocket. At this moment the conductor arrived, and the stranger, arising, burst into an impassioned protest. When he had finished, the conductor began a reproachful lecture. Atterbury, still studying abstractedly the countryside, drew out the card and handed it over. "Oh, that's different, sir", said the conductor, and led the stranger away, promising to find him a seat elsewhere.[4]

There is something pleasantly perverse about our lot. Such a reminder, at times is worth a fortune. I bought the biography of Fields one Spring in Rome at a rummage sale for fifty lire, about eight pence. The best things in life are almost free.

19

Men in search of glory; optimism is our worst enemy; find a little bad in the best of things; never give a sucker an even break — such are the contrasts and contradictions of our times, even of our lot. What I wish to pursue in the beginning is the curious way our intellectual and political history has overturned itself in recent years. We seem often to have a restlessness not of our own making. In John Berryman's warm and human poem, "Five Addresses to the Lord", we read:

> Incomprehensible to man your ways.
> May be the Devil after all exists.
> "I don't try to reconcile anything", said the poet at eighty,
> "this is a damned strange world".[5]

And Isaac Bashevis Singer remarked, in one of his delightful memoirs, "Things happen in life so fantastic that no imagination could have invented them".[6]

A damned strange world, so fantastic that no one could have invented it — such is, I suspect, the truth not only of our personal lives, but of the events of history and politics themselves, events, moods, reasons, and passions which charge our public world. The improbable, the strange, the fantastic, it seems to me anyhow, happen all about us — we are not ruled by statistics even when it seems we are.

Creatures who reach for the stars

We sometimes are weary of threats and plots, resisting and protesting and exposing everyone for what we all are, much less than we want to be. The left is after reactionaries and plots. Among the liberals, all parties, of course, must have equal rights to demonstrate and to be heard. When the noted German weekly, *Die Zeit*, celebrated its twenty-fifth anniversary, it seemed that the reasonable, fair, calm, liberal had fallen on evil days.[7] In his editorial, Marion

Gräfin Dönhoff vainly tried to revivify the liberal ideas of mutual tolerance and freedom, not just against the fascists but also against current marxism, where more than a little fascism still lives. How odd it seemed that after a mere quarter of a century, leading rational, liberal journalists, almost pleadingly, would have to defend their very philosophical and political existence against those who accuse them of being — the German was descriptive — "Wischi-Waschi-Bürger", men who merely talk but do not know how to act. "We have today men who think they can overcome the thousand-year-old problem of the exploitation of men by men in the course of a single working day . . .". The radicals of the movement make an idol of unreflecting acts, "acts done without purpose or thought, without hesitation or hindsight". Such political romantics *who are reaching for the stars*, Dönhoff concluded, "have constantly made this world unlivable. . .".

Yet, this calm and admittedly necessary liberal vision, it seems to me, however indispensable, still has failed to grasp the reasons for its own crisis in the contemporary world. Even the liberal sees himself only as a "counterweight", and not as the one who is reaching for the stars. Why have the romantics and the fanatics everywhere seemed to have gained so much inellectual and ethical impetus? The free market of ideas ("The legitimate place of liberals", Dönhoff put it, "is between all chairs") has not in fact worked well. This is the flaw of all classical liberal thought. It is theoretically indifferent to ends, the belief that such things are all merely a reaching for the stars. The importance of method and means has left the notion of goal and vision to others.

Man, nonetheless, I think, does not live by means alone. What the current anti-liberal, revolutionary moods are about is specifically the moral need of ends to justify and to satisfy. No longer is it enough to say that we must be "liberal" with regard to unknown or unknowable "sublime" ends. We vastly misinterpret our times if we assume that the essential questions, political or religious, are not about

21

ultimate meaning. They are about a *gloria* to be searched for and, hopefully, found.

The British, the Jews, and the basketball courts in Tirana

The late John Cardinal Heenan once gave a sermon in Dublin in which he said that Britain is a "post-Christian nation, a land of former believers . . . The people have not rejected Christianity — it is only that religion is no longer regarded as important or, as they say nowadays, relevant".[8] I believe myself, however, that it is not so important for religion to be relevant. This may be its greatest contemporary mistake. I believe rather it needs to be right and holy. Nor do I think that because organized religion is not recognized that we therefore are not confronted with a time that is almost overly religious, even mystical. "The reachers for the stars" have gained the day, as the German liberal well sensed. Our real problem is, in fact, the spiritual quality, the orthodoxy, as it were, of these new politico-mystical faiths.

Moreover, we see religion and politics so mixed up that religion seems one of the causes of war. The Muslims and the Jews have created much of the turmoil of recent years. Protestants and Catholics in Northern Ireland make religion seem obnoxious. Idi Amin maintains that Zionists stir up unrest in Uganda. All faiths are confronted with the counter-faith of marxism. If we take an obscure country like Albania, we suddenly see that the majority of this country is Muslim ruled by a tough marxist regime. The Albanian Communist Party several years ago began a bitter struggle against all religion, especially against Islam which is looked upon as a cause of backwardness in the country. "The struggle against religion should perhaps be judged from a more profound historical and social view", Enzo Bettiza wrote. "In a country where three-fourths of the people are Muslim, as in Albania, the religious struggle is, in the first place, against Islam and the Islamic heritage".[9]

Active atheism is seen as the common substitute for all religions, a way to separate the people from their past. This evidently "stupifies not only western observers, but also, if not more, certain exponents of the Third World, Muslim or South American. Those regimes with strong confessional bases such as Algiers or Cairo certainly cannot understand or consent to the closing of mosques in Tirana. Nor can a red-tinged Brazilian or Chilean priest approve the transformation of churches into basketball courts". Both the Jews and the Arabs are potentially in the same difficulty. Both the revolutionary and modernization elements of modern Marxism are ultimately anti-Islamic as well as anti-Jewish. Religion of any kind finds itself under some kind of pressure from other ultimate beliefs.

Sharing the liberties of the English tradition

Western thinkers of a distinctly liberal training, I believe, commonly under-estimate the strength of ideology and religion. Since their world-view can contain in itself no absolutes, neither can any one else's. Consequently, they consistently misjudge not merely the aberrations of absolute beliefs but also their power and necessity in the world. Man simply will not leave absolutes alone so that any theory which advises him to do so is bound to despair in confrontation with actual men and women.

Averell Harriman once gave a good example of this:

The actual ideological divergencies between the USSR and the USA are not based on their economic systems, but on the principles of the relation between the State and its citizens. I believe that with time, also in the USSR, they will move themselves towards the concept of individual liberty and of the legal state which we have inherited from the English tradition.[10]

This belief does not correspond with the picture the Soviet dissidents consistently picture of the strength of Soviet rule. They too see a loss of vision in Russia but they also fear an equal loss elsewhere. The essential optimism that all will somehow grow together seems to undervalue both the need of vision and the real strength of state power.

The new and specially aggressive sense of the inadequacy of man

We are, no doubt, ideologically and spiritually discontented. We know that some absolute order does exist, that it takes some kind of moral zeal and earnestness to discover it. The zeal and the sincerity are everywhere present among us. Yet, at the same time, we know that there can be false gods which can likewise be highly spiritual. We begin to suspect with John Berryman that "maybe after all the Devil exists". When we read some of the things that are being done to human life today, in its beginning and at its end, we are almost sure of it. We should not, however, devaluate too much our sense of inadequacy nor the revolutionary power it calls forth. Sir Peter Medawar was right:

> Superimposed on all particular causes of complaint is a more general cause of dissatisfaction. Bacon's belief in the cultivation of science for the "merit and emolument of life" has always been repugnant to those who have taken it for granted that comfort and prosperity imply spiritual impoverishment. But the real trouble nowadays has very little to do with material prosperity or technology or with our misgivings about the power of research and learning generally to make the world a better place. The real trouble is our acute sense of human failure and mismanagement, a new and specially aggressive sense of the inadequacy of man.[11]

Since Sir Peter wrote, however, this very "acute sense of failure" has indeed begun to make us question science itself. But material prosperity is not a sign of spiritual impoverishment, nor is it, on the other hand, the answer to man's ultimate meaning, as so many socio-religious

24

movements in the Third World seem to want to make it today.

Consequently, there is both a secular and a spiritual response to this sense of human inadequacy. Indeed, the two are somehow identified since the reason for our spiritual inadequacy is, paradoxically, the cause of our secular hope. In a way, it is striking that our deficiencies were ever considered reasons for despair rather than as gifts, which is in fact what they were. "Likewise mankind, symbolized in Israel", Rabbi David Goldberg wrote:

> is not to be regarded as the perfect crown of God's creation. Man is an incomplete creature who must struggle through the hardships and sufferings of this world towards his goal of union with God. God and man, the father and his child, will come together at the end, when man has reached spiritual maturity. And then God will be fulfilled.[12]

There is, in other words, both a reason why the Earth is incomplete and why man has a definite goal which is his alone. His incompleteness, as it were, is precisely why he begins to be, why he can ultimately accomplish something, why, finally, what he seeks is not his at all. Absolute ideologies and religions, consequently, are not destructive because they are absolute, as liberal thought too often insists on believing, but because there are *false* absolutes.

Making all humanity a success

We are, furthermore, bound up with the cosmos even in our finiteness. Contrary to the common notion of the physical scientists, who are too often prone to see no cosmic meaning to human life nor any relation between the success of human life on Earth and its place in the cosmos, I believe that one implies the other. We have, in a way, a spiritual necessity to go out of ourselves, to complete ourselves because we really are to transform the

Earth for men. Buckminster Fuller made this point in his usual vivid manner:

We are going to have to learn how to pack into a little portable electro-chemical system of about the size and weight of one large air-travel suitcase all the life supporting technology necessary to complement man's integral organic processing, with possibly an additional weekly milk-bottle full of metabolic essentials rocketed to each astronaut from his mother spacecraft, Earth. When and if humanity learns how to support human life successfully anywhere in the universe, the logistical economies of doing so will become so inherently efficient and satisfactory that then, and then alone, we may for the first time make all humanity a success both here and about our space vehicle, Earth.[13]

And yet, is this whole effort "worthwhile", will it satisfy no matter how grandiose the ultimate scale may be? Of course, it will not. The discovery of fire, of the Cape of Good Hope, of the steam engine, and the New World were no more absolute than the discovery and classification of the last star will be.

There is, then, an intense need to know that man has an ultimate value over and beyond and through what he can accomplish in the universe. This is what our contemporary revolutions and unrests are mainly about in their spiritual origins. We cannot, ultimately, be without our ultimate meaning. Jean-Marie le Blond noted that we all have the psychological experience of knowing our own value through the love and recognition of others. Without this, we cannot be saved from the despair of insignificance and inadequacy.

This elementary intersubjective experience leads us to place in question the value which humanity as a whole attributes to itself. In effect, on reflection, if humanity recognizes itself as being all alone in the dereliction of an immense universe, it will feel itself incapable of giving itself any true value. Here arises the evocation of Another capable of absolutely valorizing it.[14]

The world is, indeed, stranger and more fantastic than we could ever imagine. Even more, there is even a faint glimmer of hope that it all might make some sense after all.

Wisdom, and strength, and honour, and glory, and blessing

"Man", Arthur Miller wrote in a passage that gives these pages their title, *"is a social animal or a son of a bitch, as God and the prophets have warned since the beginning"*.[15]

God and the prophets have, more accurately warned that man is a social animal *and* a son of a bitch — at least, that is my interpretation and experience. Very seldom do we find anyone who is exclusively one *or* the other. God and the prophets have said that all men have sinned. They have also said that all men are called to glory.

It was raining on a Monday night in Rome. It was the middle of winter. A friend had told me *Messiah* was being performed by the Academia di Santa Cecilia Orchestra and Choir that evening. I had never heard *Messiah* completely as a performance before. Handel wrote it in twenty-four days in the late summer of 1741. It was first performed in Dublin, just where over two centuries later Cardinal Heenan had remarked that Britain was a post-Christian nation, a land of former believers.

Yet, I thought as I watched and listened to *Messiah* that this is precisely the kind of a thing that our age seeks — not only "The Messiah" in the traditional sense, but in the musical sense also, something that is *Gloria, Doxa,* Glory in its very presentation, something which is not a means to go somewhere else because it is already there where we want to go. The last Chorus ends in simple, powerful praise:

> Worthy is the Lamb that was slain,
> and hath redeemed us to God by his blood,
> to receive power, and riches,
> and wisdom, and strength,

and honour, and glory, and blessing.
Blessing and honour, glory and pow'r
be unto him that sitteth upon the throne,
and unto the Lamb forever.
Amen.

As I walked back home, again in the rain of the empty
streets of the Eternal City, near to midnight, near St Peter's,
across the Tiber by the Chiesa Nuova, Sant'Andrea della
Valle, the Collegio Romano, across the Corso by the Dodici
Apostoli, I thought — Yes, it is true, the Social Gospel
is not nearly enough, however important it might be.

There are things in the universe, Ye Sons of Bitches,
that are ever so strange and fantastic. They are luminous
all about you. You should, indeed, find a little bad in the
best of things, for we are all sinners. But man has need of
Glory. Our worst enemy is optimism, while some of us
see enemies everywhere. We are all Wischi-Waschi-Bürgers
with a deep sense of the inadequacy of man.

Do not think all is well on the face of this Earth, that
the Russians are all merely German liberals on their way
to becoming Englishmen or that the socialists love the
Jews or that the Muslims are happy in Tirana.

We are, alas, searchers to whom someone has given
a slightly more than even break. We are surely incomplete
creatures who have set out to know the universe. In the
end, however, we will find nothing, as God and the
prophets rightly say. For the truth is rather the opposite:
In the end, we shall be found.

Blessing and honour, glory and pow'r . . .

The sentence that now rings in my memory is rather
that of Isaac Bashevis Singer: *Things happen in life so
fantastic that no imagination could have invented them.*

This is, indeed, a damned strange world.

Praise it, Ye Sons of Bitches.

NOTES

[1] *Corriere della Sera,* 14 Marzo 1971.
[2] *La Stampa,* 26 Febbraio 1971.
[3] *W.C. Fields: His Follies and His Fortunes,* Signet, 1967, p. 77.
[4] *Ibid.,* p. 80.
[5] *Saturday Review,* 20-10-1970, p. 23.
[6] *In My Father's Court,* New York, 1966, p. 116.
[7] February 19, 1971.
[8] *Herald-Tribune,* Paris, 15 March 1971.
[9] *Corriere della Sera,* 14 Marzo 1971.
[10] *La Stampa,* 17 Marzo 1971.
[11] "On Effecting All Things Possible", *The Advancement of Science,* British Association for the Advancement of Science, September, 1969, p. 8.
[12] "The Survival of the Jewish Faith", *The Times,* London, 6 February 1971.
[13] "The Vertical Is to Live — Horizontal Is to Die", *The American Scholar,* Winter, 1969-70, p. 44.
[14] "Après le Christianisme", *Christus,* Paris, Juillet, 1968, p. 303.
[15] "When Time Had at Least a Form", *The New York Times,* 24 Jaunary 1971, p. 17.

Chapter II

ON BUILDING CATHEDRALS
AND TEARING THEM DOWN

And if we are to praise, there ought to be places in which we might do so.

Of the great English cathedrals, I have seen a few — St Paul's and Westminster Abbey, of course, Litchfield, Worcester, Durham, Salisbury, Bath Abbey, Chichester, Waltham Abbey, St Albans and Coventry. I have caught brief glimpses of York, Edinburgh and King's Chapel, have been enchanted by smaller churches such as those of Mullion or St Hilary's in Cornwall or Marylebone or the place where Burke is commemorated in Beaconsfield. On the continent, I have seen Notre Dame, Sainte Chapelle, Rheims, Rouen, Mont Saint-Michel, Cologne, Freiburg, the churches of Nüremburg and Würzburg, Bämburg and Salzburg, Toledo, Milano, St Mark's, St Nicholas in Bari, the various edifices of Florence, Palermo, Genoa, Naples and Rome. Each of these extraordinary structures, built somehow in a way I do not wholly understand by ages far poorer than our own, incited me strangely in the thoroughly unexpected way that something which need not exist at all surprises and awakens us when, contrary to our private illusions and expectations, we suddenly discover that it exists and that it is lovely.

Indeed, I prefer to know little or even nothing about

such structures before I see them for the first time. I would just as soon never have heard of Notre Dame or St Mark's at the moment I first entered them. The photographs and education itself, alas, makes this delightful sort of ignorance quite impossible. Yet, I literally knew nothing of Durham or Waltham Abbey or Santa Maria Gloriosa dei Frari or the baroque churches of Salzburg or Würzburg before I suddenly one day discovered them floating before me. The shock and glory of unexpectedly finding such buildings touches almost the peak of human experience.

The very foundations of our existence, then, are grounded in this startling realization that we do not already grasp all of reality, especially things of such exalted beauty. We cannot but be humbled by the immediate revelation of how much we have missed. And yet we are glad that, so humbled, we can now inherit what the Earth has borne to us. For we stand to all reality as we do to Durham and to Freiburg and to Litchfield when we behold them for the first time, when we are given something by the ages that we could not create or even imagine by ourselves.

Yet the cathedral that haunts me most is still Coventry. This cathedral, of course, is a very recent one, a symbol of World War II, its destructive force and man's capacity to heal again. Coventry was a familiar word in my youth. It meant quite literally the total obliteration of a human city. Nevertheless, when I actually saw Coventry several years ago, what struck me was not merely the hope that it embodied, its combination of what remained with what was new, but more especially the overwhelming realization that great and beautiful cathedrals could be built by Christians and that millions of men and women would come to see them merely because they were lovely. Coventry saved me from the sickness of so much of modern religion which believes that earnest duty and grim revolution are what praise of the Lord is all about. Somehow it seemed to me on leaving Coventry at the time that such a cathedral transcended human times and human divisions, that men really did need a beautiful place because they suddenly felt again there that worship was a normal and ordinary thing for men to do.

None the less, Coventry need not have existed, nor Durham, nor Notre Dame, nor St Peter's, for that matter. Such places, somehow, were beyond the category of what I have called "need". John Cage, in a delightful essay he entitled, "Diary: How to improve the world (You will only make it worse), Continued, 1966", said: "Bad politics (Souvtchinsky) produced good art. But of what use is good art? (John said he could imagine a world without it and that there is no reason to think it would not be a better one)".[1] All civilization, as well as all religion, ultimately rests upon this truth that we do not "need" beautiful things to be good. Beautiful things belong precisely to that category of reality which is, as the Greeks first taught, beyond necessity. They are precisely "unnecessary". This is their glory.

Thus man is, in fact, that being in the universe who can build unnecessary things and make them beautiful. And conversely, the ultimate sign of barbarism is to burn down something that is truly lovely — and to burn it down in the name of man himself, as if this act would somehow ennoble him further. Indeed, even more, the final mark of incivility is never to build a beautiful thing in the first place. This is why in the end, all barbarism, even all heresy, comes to attack beauty in the name of bread. In other words, the most radical contempt for the poor is to proclaim that they need bread more than beauty, that they literally do, in fact, live by bread alone.

Samuel Johnson in the Hebrides

In a used book store over on Clement Street in San Francisco, I once came across a second-hand copy of Samuel Johnson's *A Journey to the Western Islands of Scotland*.[2] This was a trip Johnson, accompanied by his Scottish friend, James Boswell, took through Scotland and the Hebrides in the late summer and early autumn of 1773. At this time, Scotland had just fallen under the complete control of the English and seemed to Johnson barren, depopulated, and backward. As he rode from town to town, Johnson noted the customs, the language, the manners, the peculiarities of these sturdy people whom he seemed to like. He marked the weather, the scenery, the food, the housing, the animals, the farming, the working conditions.

But what appalled Johnson most was the evidence he saw of the wholesale neglect and destruction of the Scottish churches during the Reformation. On August 19, for example, he was in St Andrews where he arose in the morning to "perambulate" the city, as he quaintly put it, only to "survey the ruins of ancient magnificence". He continued:

The cathedral, of which the foundations may be still traced, and a small part of the wall is standing, appears to have been a spacious and majestic building, not unsuitable to the primacy of the Kingdom. Of the architecture, the poor remains can hardly exhibit it, even to an artist, a sufficient specimen. It was demolished, as is well known, in the tumult of Knox's Reformation.[3]

Then, on August 26, Johnson came to Elgin where he stopped at an inn about noon for dinner. Even though this inn was supposed to be the best in town, the food was inedible, though Johnson attributed this to lack of travellers in such parts rather than to any defect in Scottish cookery.

After this unsatisfying dinner, Johnson then came upon the ruins of the local church. "The ruins of this cathedral of Elgin afforded us another proof of the waste of the Reformation".[4] But, he sadly continued, Elgin was not destroyed so much by "the tumultuous violence of Knox" but was "more shamefully suffered to delapidate by deliberate robbery and frigid indifference". Indeed, not unlike those Popes who mined the Colosseum and the Pantheon to build other palaces and churches, the lead on the cathedrals of Elgin and Aberdeen was stripped to finance the Scottish army by selling it to the Dutch. "I hope every reader will rejoice that this cargo of sacrilege was lost at sea", Johnson acidly remarked.[5]

Furthermore, he continued, the English were not much better:

> Let us not, however, make too much haste to despise our neighbours. Our own cathedrals are mouldering by unregarded delapidation. It seems to be part of the despicable philosophy of the time to despise monuments of sacred magnificence, and we are in danger of doing that deliberately, what the Scots did not do but in the unsettled state of an imperfect constitution.[6]

And Johnson's final remark is both poignant and prophetic, " . . . Those who had once uncovered the cathedrals never wished to cover them up again . . .".

On building and tearing down

Why should we build cathedrals? We want a sacred time and a sacred space, where we can celebrate, when we can pray and sing and dance simply because that is what men do when they discover joy, what they also do when they suffer sorrow. Mircea Eliade noted that sacred space — the temple, the basilica, the cathedral —

> makes possible the "founding of the world": where the sacred manifests itself in space, the real unveils itself, the world comes into existence. But the irruption of the sacred does not only project a fixed point into the formless fluidity of profane space, a centre into chaos; it also effects a break in the plane, that is, it opens communication between cosmic planes (between earth and heaven) and makes possible ontological passages from one mode of being to another.[7]

The cathedral makes the secular world possible; the secular world makes the cathedral into a vision beyond itself.

Where this is not vision, the people live only in dullness and greyness.

Why do men believe the temples should be torn down? Clement of Alexandria preserved for us the classic argument:

> Zeno, the founder of the Stoic school, says in his book on the *Republic* that men ought not to erect temples or to make images, since no work of man's hands is worthy of the gods. He does not shrink from pressing his point in these very words: "There will be no need to erect temples: a temple which is not precious and holy must be counted as nothing, and no work of masons and mechanics is precious or holy".[8]

So only God can make a temple precious and holy, anything that man can do, the works of the masons and the mechanics, must count for nothing. Therefore, to remain holy we should not build temples; therefore we should tear them down.

The new St Mary's

The second game of the World Series of Baseball was played on a Sunday in early October. As it was the day before Columbus Day (October 12), San Francisco was holding its huge annual parade, a parade originating in the recognition the City of St Francis gives to its citizens who originated in the Land of Columbus and Assisi. Beginning about one o'clock in the Civic Centre, the parade marched down Polk Street to O'Farrell, to Kearney, then down Columbus Avenue to the Italian national Church of Sts Peter and Paul on Washington Square in North Beach where the reviewing stand was located.

I decided the parade was more important than even such a serious game, so I walked down to the corner of Geary and Polk in time to see the Mayor (himself, appropriately, an Italian) pass by, followed by innumerable high school

c

marching bands — Ygnacio Valley, Piedmont Hills, St Francis of Mountain View, Balboa, Samuel Ayer, Concord — military and ROTC units, sheriffs' posses, baton twirlers, mostly tiny girls under eight, drum and bugle corps, unicyclists, clowns, floats, political candidates, police and fire department officials. I had almost forgotten how wonderful a parade could be — the human condition, men and women and children in their decorations and symbols passing us by. Pageantry too, I thought, is totally unnecessary. Yet still, thank God for Columbus Day Parades in the City of St Francis by the Bay! Is it the unnecessary things that we count most often in our memories and dreams? I surely think so.

Afterwards I caught a bus back to the University. A student from one of my political theory classes was on the bus. As we passed below the new St Mary's Cathedral, I remarked, perhaps for the hundredth time since I had first seen it, how beautiful a structure this really was. I had been walking all over this city during the previous few weeks and months. I had seen it from all different angles and places since, one day downtown crossing O'Farrell Street, I suddenly looked up the street and realized it really did exist magnificently against the skyline.

But my young friend then promptly told me that the cathedral should not have been built, especially as there were slums in the area. The money would have been better given to the poor. Further, it was merely a monument to comfort middle-class Catholics, to make them feel nice. Alas, the middle-class Catholics I knew mostly bitched about the cathedral because it cost them so much money, a money better spent on living expenses. Paradoxically, it was the Jews and Protestants who said to me, as Barry Hibbin said to me the summer after it opened, on a sailboat in the middle of the Bay, "It is a stunning success, a most glorious thing for the city". Did the inhabitants of old Ely and Lincoln and Chartes, I wonder, complain about the cost and the waste? How do you call man out of his everyday routine and narrowness?

36

I myself believe this cathedral may very well be the most beautiful building in America. And so I chided my young and earnest friend, shades of Zeno and Samuel Johnson, "Why are you all young and presumably radical students always stoics and puritans?" How little they know about the intellectual structures of the enthusiasms of the past! I thought to myself. Then aloud, "Don't you know the poor have more need of beauty than of bread? That you show utter contempt for the poor if you forbid man to build beautiful things?"

Yet he was unmoved by my rhetoric. Can he really believe, I wondered, that it really would be better were such a thing not to exist? I guess I have never recovered from the experience so common to me in Europe where the poorest of families will take you familiarly into the local cathedral, show you its beauties, and thereby let you know that it is also in some way a part of their lives too, a gift from the centuries to them and to all men.

The first Mass in the new St Mary's

St Mary's Cathedral in San Francisco was opened for its first Sunday Masses on October 18, 1970. Somehow I knew I had to be there for this first day of a cathedral in which, I faintly hoped, there would be Masses for a thousand years. Do other men still have such wishes, I wondered, that things beginning in our own generation will still be going on so long down the ages? My life in Rome, I suppose, has somehow corrupted me into believing this is quite a normal and ordinary sentiment. And yet I believe in the year 3000 as well as in the year 2000. And I am somehow very tired of our intellectual classes who really do not believe over much in tomorrow morning.

So I again walked down Eddy Street through the Fillmore (along the way I sadly noted again wonderful old San Francisco Victorian houses being torn down and being replaced by social legislation, up-to-date, public authority, square cement block flats in the name of, for God's sake, "concern for the poor") to Laguna, to Cleary Street. Cleary Street is a brief street, the continuation of O'Farrel. It is the best possible way to approach this cathedral, through its fountains and flowers and shrubbery and its very modern designs. I thought again, the houses of men do not have to be ugly. The ten-thirty Mass was just ending when I entered the cathedral for the first time.

There is no way to prepare someone for the breathtaking beauty of the inside of this church. I had had an inkling that this was to be an experience of a very moving kind. My friend Gerald Adams of the *Examiner* had been on tour inside the cathedral a couple of months before. He told me later, and this somehow had touched me more because he is a Jew in his family background, that he wept at seeing it for the first time. So did I when I left the cathedral after about half an hour, not realizing quite what was wrong with my eyes. How astonished we are at ourselves when we remember what beauty can do to us.

Perhaps a thousand people were at Mass. There was quiet and awe inside. The ceiling, the way your eyes automatically rise to the top of the structure, the sense of geometric form, the corner windows that make the city itself such a lovely city, somehow part of the building, the stained-glass windows, the cross over the altar — I hardly knew what to look at. I walked about for a while, went to each of the windows, hardly comprehending how the city, so lively in itself, could also be here inside. I knew I would come here often and stay a long while.

After the ten-thirty Mass, I noticed something I had never quite experienced in any American church before. The congregation spontaneously rose and slowly, reverently, yet talking too, scattered throughout the cathedral, to the altar, to the windows, the pylons, some merely staying in their seats gazing at the altar, the stained-glass windows, the city. The priests were all out of the sacristy, themselves explaining and answering questions, as if they too could hardly believe it really existed before them.

I was not quite sure why all of this struck me so much until I walked down Van Ness Avenue for a cup of coffee between Masses. As I went by Old St Mark's Lutheran Church across the street from the cathedral, by the lovely Gothic of the First Unitarian Church on Franklin and Geary, the Hamilton Square Baptist Church across the street, I recalled from my recent walks that within ten blocks of the cathedral there must be twenty or thirty churches and synagogues of various denominations. American churches, Protestant, Catholic and Jewish, are built for their congregations. Indeed, we all have a constitutional right to our own diversities. In fact, probably it was our divisions that introduced our constitutional right to have them.

Yet for all this, you do not just "drop in" to an American church as you do into the great European churches. For the most part, we quite literally need to be taken and made welcome by a neighbour. But suddenly in Zim's Restaurant, of all places, I realised the meaning of what I had just seen in St Mary's was. Here is a cathedral so lovely that it transcends divisions. Though it is "Catholic", it is a beautiful structure which belongs to San Francisco and to the world. Every one belongs there because somehow men have created a sacred place where the holy drops into the midst of this city which, in its own way, has been searching for civic holiness for so long. For San Francisco is a place tinged with both worldliness and mysticism, the Barbary Coast and the Flower Children, Haight-Ashbury and the Golden Gate Bridge, which you can either walk across or jump from. The theology of the cathedral has long suspected that you cannot long have, and remain sane, the one without the other, the mysticism without the wordliness, the wordliness without the mysticism.

Nonetheless, the modern stoics (who protested that the cathedral should not have been built) and the modern radicals (who think the money should have been given to the poor) are right, of course. San Francisco and the world do not *need* this monument to lead the "good' and "moral" life. To the men who believe sincerely that the humble need only bread, St Mary's will be a sin and a scandal. The purists fought hard not to build it. And the good Archbishop who built it hesitated to dedicate it with formal celebration because he knew that, in the climate of our times of virtuous opinion, someone would probably have attempted to blow it up, blow it up in the name of religion and virtue and sincerity. For St Mary's to house Mass and San Francisco for a thousand years, it must be first loved and cherished. Otherwise, in the name of God, it will be destroyed.

The ages, nevertheless, will be grateful for this building, even though our generations may not be able to protect it from the bombs of our zealots, as the French were not able to protect the Abbey of Cluny during the Revolution. Indeed, it is truly unnecessary. It is only beautiful. This is what civilization is all about.

The bridges and the visibility

The wise English Dominican, Dom Iltud Evans, wrote: "San Francisco is a city that is made for monuments. The setting of hills and ocean, the rhythm of the bridges that span the Bay, give it a character that is dramatic and altogether its own. It calls for an architecture that can match its surprises".[9] And you cannot pay for or march for or even pray for surprises. They merely come somehow crashing into the midst of our city and our lives like St Mary's on the first Sunday it was open to the world.

So Zeno was right, "No work of masons and mechanics is precious and holy". And the protestors are right, the Archbishop should have forgotten St Mary's, beautiful St Mary's on Geary and Gough. The puritans are right. The lovely English and Scottish churches were monuments to vanity and display, good only to be stripped bare in the name of the Lord. And my student friend was right too. We should not build a beautiful cathedral in the midst of slums. It is all so perfectly logical and reasonable.

Yet, this is surely insane.

Why should we build cathedrals? Why should we tear them down?

Bad politics makes good art indeed. The building of St Mary's Cathedral in San Francisco may well have been bad politics in today's mad world. Yet it is splendid art, a beautiful, sacred place. It has become, as Gerald Adams remarked, "A new focal point for San Francisco", a place to be seen from afar, to be seen close up, a place whose very visibility takes us out of ourselves from wherever we may chance to see it in the city.[10] A new focal point where the holy falls amidst the city; a sacred art; bad politics; tear it down — if ultimately we are forced to choose between grimness and loveliness, let us somehow still choose loveliness.

How to improve the world? Will you only make it worse? St Mary's Cathedral now exists. It comes out of nothingness. And like all that once begins in nothingness, it wonderfully surprises us. St Mary's Cathedral has begun the rest of its days.

Quod visum placet

The day before the cathedral opened, I walked through the lovely square plaza that surrounds its base. I asked a young man if any door was by chance open. He told me in French he did not speak English. He was from Paris, visiting the States for a month. In my worst French (I have no other kind) I tried to tell him about this place, when it would open, what it was. This young Frenchman was symbolic — as I sometimes think all things are. The world already wants to see San Francisco — even in the land of Chartres and Rouen and Rheims and Sacre-Cœur, word of

41

the surprise of St Mary's will soon begin to be heard. This young Frenchman began a flood and was a symbol, at least to me, of what was to come.

So when you come to San Francisco, walk there. Go quietly through the Strybing Arboretum in Golden Gate Park, do not miss the wonderful dark Monterey Cypress there as you look back from the fountain, on a little knoll against the deep blue sky. I think it is the loveliest tree in all the world. Stroll up Telegraph Hill and watch the ships and the sailboats and the ferries all drifting against the Marin shore and Angel Island and the Bridges. Amble through the Presidio and thank the Army for keeping it. And do not forget the dead buried there. Do not neglect to walk across Golden Gate Bridge and wonder how it could have been built at all.

And sit in the park across from Grace Cathedral on Nob Hill, take some time in Portsmouth Square, and behold the gigantic buildings from Old St Mary's Square. Climb Russian Hill, eat something in Chinatown, and again on Fisherman's Wharf. Clement Street is very charming, as is Union Street and Chestnut Street. Wind down Lombard Street which thinks it is the crookedest in the world. Take a cable car, and slowly walk Upper Broadway to watch the Bay and the beautiful houses. See the worldliness of Lower Broadway, wade in the surf of Ocean Beach in the evening to discover, in the West, why the Indians long ago called it the Sundown Sea. And when you finally come back to St Mary's, wonder if indeed there is any glory that is like this.

In the end, there need be no St Mary's, no San Francisco, no Bridges, no bay, no earth, no sky, nothing at all.

But it does now exist, St Mary's. And it is beautiful.

NOTES

[1] *A Year From Monday,* Wesleyan University Press, 1967, p. 60.
[2] Boston, Houghton-Mifflin, 1965.

[3] *Ibid.,* p. 3.
[4] *Ibid.,* p. 17.
[5] *Ibid.,* p. 18.
[6] *Ibid.,* p. 18.
[7] *The Sacred and the Profane,* Harper Torchbooks, 1957, p. 63.
[8] In J. von Armin, Stoicorum Veterum, Fragmenta, Vol. I, in Ernest Barker, *From Alexander to Constantine,* Clarendon Press, 1959, p. 26.
[9] *Oakland Voice,* 6 March 1968.
[10] *San Francisco Examiner,* 10 October 1970.

Chapter III

ON THE CHRISTIAN LOVE OF ANIMALS

God is to be praised and there ought to be places in which we, men in search of glory, might sing. Yet, on this Green Earth, there are also myriads of animals. I saw a TV documentary recently which said there may be a hundred billion birds alone on Earth. And the Lord knows how many spiders and toads. What is the relation of all these things, of God and the funny animal we foolishly call *rational* and the mutts we get annoyed at for nipping at our heels?

To be human is to be concerned about animals. Man is the social *animal*, that animal which laughs, as Aristotle once said. Very often, our notion of this animality in us is looked upon as something rather evil and frightening. Animal images are often used as descriptions of our actions at their humanly worst. Animals, acting like animals, are functioning well and properly, doing what they are made to do. Lacking better terminology, perhaps, we say that men at their worst are "bestial". Plato, in a famous image in *The Republic*, warned of that wild, untamed, reckless animal deep within us revealed by our dreams and too often by our actions. In an oft-quoted phrase, Thomas Hobbes claimed that "Man is a wolf to man", whereas wolves are apparently quite kindly beasts. And Descartes even proposed that animals were machines because he could hypothesize that they might be.

But the subject of animals, our treatment and use of

them, and our relation to them has suddenly been repropounded from a number of diverging sources. Generally, in the Judaeo-Christian tradition, animals were held to be under man's "dominion". This meant that the animal kingdom was for man's use and well-being. Men were not to be sacrificed to animals. Currently, however, the ecology school warns us that we must not tamper further with our biophysical environment. E.F. Schumacher, in his widely discussed *Small is Beautiful,* insists that we must learn to live with the animals again, to stress permanent and rooted things. "For man to put himself into a wrongful relationship with animals, and particularly those long domesticated by him", Schumacher wrote,

> has always, in all traditions, been considered a horrible and infinitely dangerous thing to do. There have been no sages or holy men in our or in anybody else's history who were cruel to animals or who looked upon them as *nothing but* utilities, and innumerable are the legends and stories which link sanctity as well as happiness with a loving kindness towards lower creatures.[1]

Peter Singer and Thomas Regan are intellectual leaders of a vast revisionist movement known as "Animal Liberation", which purports to carry the Black, Gay, and Woman's Liberation Movements to their logical conclusions. They insist that we take a look at the vast amount of pain we inflict on animals by our factory farms, our hunting practices, our zoo keeping facilities, our treatment of pets, our experimentations, our use of pelts, eggs, and meat.

English Roman Catholics, furthermore, have a study group devoted to animals, a group which maintains a kiosk of information at Lourdes. They also publish a journal, not unexpectedly called *The Ark.* And the proliferation of health food stores and Buddhist monks all over the West attests to the arrival of a new ethic and attitude towards non-human life. We may very well be at the state of a total restructuring of society that would follow from our accepting what Albert Schweitzer called "The

45

ethic of life", life in men, animals, insects and plants.

In this context, I wish to raise the question, paradoxical as it sounds, of the Christian love of animals. Oddly, I have learned that in our society, no two subjects are more emotionally explosive than criticism of animals and criticism of abortion. At first sight, I never felt the two were particularly connected, but now I am inclined to think that they are. Indeed, I suspect that the animal liberation movements may be the best allies the abortion critics can have. This has not been apparent so far since most Christians have felt the animal liberationists prefer animals to humans. But this need not be the case. A growing respect for all life cannot help but result in a respect for human life in all its forms. And this too may well be a positive thing in the attempts to improve the diets of men all over the world.

There are, however, levels of theory and levels of manners and practice. Christianity has not neglected the animals. In the Gospel of Luke, Christ asks, "Are not five sparrows sold for two pennies? And not one of them is forgotten before God . . . Fear not; you are of more value than many sparrows" (12:6-7). The notion of human dominion did not mean, then, that single sparrows were not within God's concern, even though men and women might be of more value than a flight of sparrows. And we read in *The Little Flowers of St Francis of Assisi:*

A certain youth had caught one day a great number of turtledoves; and as he was taking them to market he met St Francis, who, having singular compassion for these gentle creatures, looked at the doves with eyes of pity, and said to the youth: "Oh, good youth, I pray thee give me these gentle birds, to which in the Holy Scriptures chaste and humble and faithful souls are compared; and do not let them fall into the hands of cruel men who would kill them".[2]

What, then, are the implications of a Christian love of animals within this broader context of concern for life, animal liberation, and the fact that men are worth more than many sparrows?

Manners: human and animal

To place myself firmly in the context of human manners rather than on the more metaphysical issues that will arise later, I am frankly biased about animals — unfavourably biased. Let me begin by noting that I am not amused by friends' furry spaniels or their slinky cats jumping all over me in what is wildly called "enthusiastic greeting", when I am invited into their homes. "Love me, love my dog", I definitely consider an immoral principle. In my jaundiced view, it must either be, "Love me, contain your pooch", or else, "Love your poodles, look for a new friend". When Aristotle said that man was a "rational animal", he at least meant that the worst of us is better than the best of them. Thus I fully admit to receiving an occult pleasure every time I see W. C. Fields' famous remark, "Anyone who hates dogs and children can't be all bad". Now, I happen to like most children. Some, to be sure, are quite obnoxious little critters. I am no absolute idealist. Babies are already quite human, as Augustine once tried to describe. But still, I do not consider Fields' law to be one whit less valid for all that.

Further, I confess, along with any honest believer, that I have as much trouble as anyone else in observing the Ten Commandments, not to mention those Two Great Summaries which contain the Law and the Prophets. However, I have no difficulty whatsoever in obeying the admonition in the *Book of Leviticus*, which reads:

> Every swarming thing that swarms upon the earth is an abomination; it shall not be eaten, whatever goes on its belly, and whatever goes on all fours, and whatever has many feet . . . you shall not eat for they are abominations (11:41-42).

But *no way* are you going to catch me munching caterpillars, night-crawlers, hornets or ants — even if the

47

Japanese do cover them with chocolate. In my book, there is absolutely no need for a special revelation on these matters.

I do like baby chickens, ducklings, calves, lambs, and even an occasional hound. I can well enough understand the Parable of the Lost Sheep. And I am glad one of the Lord's messianic titles is that of the Good Shepherd. Also, I like tropical fish aquariums, all lit up in a dark room, bubbling madly, green, rocky, transparent. I like them, that is, provided I do not have to clean them. I could never shoot a horse through the head with a rifle after it broke its leg, as my uncle on the farm did. Even at the time, I sensed this meant that he knew about animals and cared for them, while I did not. I was only worried about my feelings, not the horse's.

Probably, it is not wholly wrong to project human norms on to the animals — "Thou shalt not kill" — even Isaiah does this when he warned: "He who slaughters an ox is like him who kills a man . . ." (66:3). Yet, there are considerable dangers too — I shall come back to Calcutta — in such projections. The anti-vivisectionists and the Society for the Prevention of Cruelty to Animals constantly stand on the verge of inhumanity, even though they do have a point. We are not, as *Genesis* implied, to prefer animals to men, even if we do name them. They are for our use, enjoyment and life. There are, for example, more horses in America today than at any time in our history, very few of which are intended for food (except perhaps for pet food!) or for work, though quite a few do end up as meat. When I lived in Ghent in Belgium, the Sunday night special was sliced horse meat, which I ate with gusto until I found out what it was.

Priorities

Animals are good in themselves, fascinating in their variety, breeds and habits. But in a crunch, anyone who sacrifices man to animals, however this be done, is idolatrous. Thus, I am spiritually far closer to the Hindu respect for all life than I am to the Christian or liberal or secularist who approves, say, abortion or compulsory euthanasia, while joining the Sierra Club to preserve mountain goats, condors or giant redwoods. I am in this also much closer to classical Marxism which was very dogmatic about what this planet was for, namely, man.

The Old Testament bloody sacrifices, as well as those of other ancient religions (Tacitus tells us Roman augurs killed chickens before battle to read their entrails for signs of approval or disapproval) thus destroyed animals, perfect, unblemished lambs and bullocks as a sign of the Lord's total domination over his creation and our recognition of it. It is indeed interesting to speculate why the current orthodox Israeli have not rebuilt the Temple in Jerusalem and reinaugurated the sacrifices of the Old Law. Thus, when we remember Abraham and Christ, the problems of man, animals and God become ever more profound. The contemporary concern we are witnessing in our sophisticated world for animal welfare and suffering is not, I think, without its serious import.

James Fellows, in *The Atlantic*, called animal liberation the "Radical Chic of 1976".[3] Nonetheless, I sometimes suspect that we are watching nothing less than the overturn of the place of man in nature. Peter Singer extends the questions of the rights of liberty and life to animals. Using the criterion of similarity of awareness and sense perceptiveness, he believes that we must begin to consider the way we make animals suffer, the way we use them.[4] We cannot any longer laugh off as merely absurd those parts of Scripture that saw the worship of animals and nature as the greatest enemy of the Lord. For, as I have suggested already, this whole subject has of late become something of a sign of contemporary moral contradiction. We do well to think about it more explicitly. And sometimes our values are so confused. We feed our pet animals in the United States better meat and diet than a large percentage of the world's human population receives. And we are not the only guilty ones here. Indeed, several years ago, *The Wall Street Journal* carried a series of articles on the aged in the United States. The surveyors were astounded to find that many elderly people eat dog food because it is nutritious and relatively cheap.

I was in New Zealand not so long ago. Historically, in those islands, only wingless birds existed because they had no natural predators. This lack of other animals seems to have been due to certain deficiencies in the soil. When rabbit and deer were introduced, along with fertilizer and farm animals, they became pests — by human standards. So these animals had to be severely controlled. Some stories even tell of romantics who wanted to introduce the lion and tiger into those distant islands. Their famous rainbow trout were imported also ˆinto New Zealand streams.

So this is the first thing I should like to insist upon in the context of animal liberation: the right relation between man and beast cannot be one that is based upon the questioning of the primacy of man in nature. We may well need to change our relation to the animals. But the reason for this is not that we cannot find a difference between animals and men. The balanced diet of our pets is not more important than that of our old or that of people in other lands.

My point, however, is *not* that I think that the reason why the old or the hungrier peoples are in the state they are is *because* we feed our pets with good meat. Indeed, Herman Kahn rightly suggested that it is *because* we raise great amounts of grain for animals and pets that the world has a constant reserve for times of crisis.[5] More and more, there is room for both men and animals in a balanced system. Thus the whole world will be soon enough exactly like New Zealand, deciding what and how many animals it desires. But it is about the human condition that any such decision should be made, with recognition of the real value and worth of animals for what it is.

A couple of years ago, an old friend called inviting me to dinner and to a lecture in the Masonic Auditorium on Nob Hill in San Francisco by Mr Gerald Durrell. "Who is Gerald Durrell?" I ignorantly inquired. "Oh, you don't know? He writes good books about zoos and animals. Our youngest daughter has read them all and insists on hearing him". And the lecture was interesting. I again have to be grateful to the enthusiasm of my young friends. The burden of Mr. Durrell's rather short talk and film was to present the case for his zoo on the Isle of Jersey in the English Channel. Durrell is concerned especially with preserving species that are supposedly endangered. In itself, this is a worthy enough project, and I have no particular quarrel with it.

However, I have plenty of reservations. Mr. Durrell's main argument for his effort was this: if we spend so much money and energy in preserving, say, a Rembrandt, we should do the same to preserve an endangered species of animal, which after all is God's work of art. The clinching argument was always a form of "Once gone, gone forever". What is of interest in all this, however, is what is left unspoken. We know perfectly well that before man ever appeared on the Earth, myriads of species disappeared from the Earth. Just how absolute, in other words, is this evidently self-evident law that no species must ever be allowed to disappear? At what cost do we save them? If we save them, are we preventing some further modification?

In all of this, I believe, a rather striking contradiction exists. On the one hand, we are told that the survival of animals is up to us, presumably the fittest animal by an older definition, or we would not still be about. On the other hand, it is intimated that the preservation of animals and plants and termites really conditions our survival so that we cannot do too much with the Earth for our own welfare because it is too fragile. One must wonder in what sense we can really speak of evolution anymore. In any case,

D

either nature is still evolving, in which case we should not worry because what does not survive, for whatever reason, is simply unfit; or else, man is now completely in charge of nature, to define what and how many animals and bugs and plants like poison ivy and roses and dandelions should survive. In other words, everything is now a zoo, a Chinese garden, a farm, or a playing field. This is why Durrell was forced to make his most telling argument for the preservation of rare animal species through an analogy with art, something that is beyond the use of categories.

With a niece and nephew, I was once invited to attend a double feature — *Jesus Christ, Superstar* and *Bless the Beasts and Children*. Jesus Christ Superstar, of course, amidst rather good music, could not figure out who he was, God, man, or both. In the second film, the beasts and the children were in a similar predicament. Penned buffalo were shot for sport by rather grim hunters with high-powered rifles in the movie. A group of children were appalled by this. They believed these buffalo were free spirits and needed liberation. The humans who shot them were pictured as beasts. All of this is especially curious if we can recall Aristotle's remark in *The Politics* where he said that someone who does not naturally belong to and live in the city is either a beast or a god. Evidently today the division in the great chain of being has never been more obscure. I see few more graphic signs of a profound confusion among us than when a Jesus Christ Superstar cannot figure out where he belongs in the levels of being, while children see buffalo to be better than men.

In this connection, moreover, James Fellows reported:

Last year . . . the *New York Times* reported that high school students in the area were sabotaging their biology labs; one fifteen-year-old girl from Westchester County rescued "the rat on the bad diet" from a classroom nutrition experiment and nursed it back to health at home . . . "Their view of life", a teacher reported, "is so much broader than mine. They don't like life washed

52

away, whether it's a dog or an elephant or an amœba. That to me is fantastic".[6]

Thus Gods, men, animals, bugs, plants and amœba are all mixed up. And if we recall biological engineering and the DNR, we feel we soon are to break the link between inanimate nature and life. Evidently everything is everything else — the great project of the medieval alchemist has almost succeeded.

Dominion over the works of thy hands

This brings me back to Calcutta. A couple of years ago, I spent some days there. Just like every other westerner who has ever been in that city, I was appalled by the emaciated cows wandering all about the city. If there is ever a place that needs the meditation on *Genesis*, it is Calcutta. Yet as I walked those streets, streets that so shock one that he is hardly able to see what is there, I began to wonder if the Christian's notion of man's place in creation will not eventually make the Hindu notion of the reverence for all life possible, indeed practical. The paradox of the most affluent society killing untold human foetuses while spending enormous sums on pet food and zoos, alongside the Hindu society needing more food but letting cattle and monkeys roam at will, seemed too startling. Added to this is the fact, as Herman Kahn also indicated, that India is in fact a very rich country in terms of resources and agricultural potential, that its problems are its political choices and attitudes.[7]

In such light, surely something like the Psalm 8 means more than we traditionally give it credit for:

> Yet thou hast made him a little less than God,
> and dost crown him with glory and honour.
> Thou hast given him dominion over the works of thy hands;
> thou hast put all things under his feet,

all sheep and oxen, and also the beasts of the field,
the birds of the air, the fish of the sea,
whatever passes along the paths of the sea.

Someday we shall all probably be vegetarian, if not
"mineralitarian", that is, people whose food is largely
created directly from component parts without passing
through the animal cycle or even the vegetable cycle.[8] I
believe the animal cycle is for our use in our present state
of "evolution", but it will pass away. We forget that practically all the animal flesh we eat comes from creatures
largely "created" in our agricultural colleges and corporate
laboratories.

C.S. Lewis used to ask (I believe in the *Four Loves*) about
the friendship or love of animals. His point was a good one.
The more we are with an animal, the more we individualize
it by our care, the less it is "animal". The apocalyptic end
of *Isaiah,* so many times painted by the medievals and by
the American primitive painter, Edward Hicks, says:

The wolf and the lamb shall feed together,
the lion shall eat straw like the ox;
and dust shall be the serpent's food.
They shall not hurt or destroy in all my holy mountain,
says the Lord (65:25).

Many such things, of course, already happen in any good
zoo. The peace of animals depends, as Thomas Aquinas
held, upon the condition and care of men, their reverence
for life, their technology, their sense of priorities. Animals
are to be loved. Their preservation is not unlike a museum
that preserves an El Greco.

Yet our hierarchy of values must be clear. And more
especially the reasons for it. One human baby is worth the
whole of the animal kingdom, even though the same baby
delights in chicks and ducks and geese and, yes, hound dogs.
We must not continue to create a modern Moloch in which
we sacrifice babies to Baal or biology. It is all right to
sacrifice animals to the Lord and to our needs — even

54

though the day is probably fast coming when, as in our faith, the bloody victim will be replaced by an unbloody one, when we will realize the progress only in retrospect, when we will insist on living quite healthily without eating animals, as most nutritionists insist that we can do.

In the Fifth Book of the *Histories* of Tacitus, he recounted the Roman version of the capture of Jerusalem.

> Moyses . . . gave them a novel form of worship, opposed to all that is practised by other men. Things sacred with us, with them have no sanctity, while they allow what with us is forbidden . . . They slay the ram, seemingly in derision of Hammon, and they sacrifice the ox, because the Egyptians worship it as Apis . . .
>
> Prodigies had occurred, which this nation, prone to superstition, but hating all religious rites, did not deem it lawful to expiate by offering and sacrifice. There had been hosts joining battle in the skies,, the fiery gleam of arms, the temple illuminated by a sudden radiance from the clouds.
>
> The doors of the inner shrine were suddenly thrown open, and a voice of more than mortal tone was heard to cry that the Gods were departing . . . Some few put a fearful meaning on these events, but in most there was a firm persuasion, that in the ancient records of their priests there was contained a prediction of how at this very time the East was to grow powerful, and rulers, coming from Judea, were to acquire universal empire.[9]

For Tacitus, of course, these universal rulers were Vespasian and Titus. Matthew, using a very similar description of the scene on Golgotha, believed it was Someone Else (27:51-54). Titus then destroyed the place of bloody sacrifice in 70 AD, while Matthew cited a Roman centurion as saying, "This surely was the Son of God". Gods and men, animals, plants and minerals . . . The destiny of the Earth is for it to be a garden within the City of God in which we are to walk in the cool of the evening and converse with the Lord amidst his creatures.

The New Zealand poet, James K. Baxter, wrote:

> Brief is the visiting angel. In the corridors of hunger
> Our lives entwined suffer the common ill:
> Living and dying, breathing and begetting.
> Meanwhile on maimed gravestones under towering
>   fennel
> Moves the bright lizard, sunloved, basking in
> The moment of animal joy.[10]

When the animals no longer suffer it means that the natural cycles of eating and being eaten will cease. The beasts will be cared for. But while the suffering of animals can and should be transformed, we humans nonetheless shall still know suffering in our finitude and in our fallenness. For our lot and theirs are not ultimately identical.

Some doubt God because we, his creatures, are not all the same. There are those who think that Fido and the buffalo and the earthworm, which Albert Schweitzer put back into the ground after a rain, should share our immortality. And for too many, Belsen and the abortion clinics and the poor in Calcutta are of less significance than the death of the last passenger pigeon. But it is not so. Indeed, to make it so is still idolatry, sacrificing to Moloch. The ancient sins are still our own.

Yet, pets are pets, and we should care for them. For this is what their destiny is to be. But still the animals are companions of a sort, co-dwellers in this niche of space we paradoxically call home. The twenty-first *fioretto* continues:

> And St Francis went and made nests for all (the turtle-doves); and they took to their nests, and began to lay eggs, and hatched them without fear before the eyes of the brothers; and they were as tame and as familiar with St Francis and all the other brothers as if they had been domestic fowls always accustomed to be fed by them and they would not depart until St Francis with his blessing gave them leave to go.

56

The *Fioretti* of St Francis are not inspired. Yet, especially today, I sometimes wonder about these legends. St Francis was, however, a Christian. For him the animals always led to God. They too somehow asked for a blessing. Anyone who hates dogs and children cannot be all bad. Bless the Beasts and Children. Thou hast given him dominion over the works of thy hands. Animals too suffer. Brief is the visiting angel. Prodigies abound which this nation did not deem it expedient to expiate by offering and sacrifice. Love me, love my dog. "Look at the birds of the air: they neither sow nor reap nor gather into barns, and yet your heavenly Father feeds them. Are you not of more value than they?" (Mt 6:26).

We learn to love animals as Christians. You, mortal men, are of more value than they. And yet, they are beautiful, even the ladybugs, lizards, tarantulas, caterpillars, as well as the swallows which go back to Capistrano, to a place in which the Brothers of Francis in 1776 built a mission on the shores of the vast Pacific.

Nevertheless, if we are to be friends: *Contain your dog.*

Something of the Law and the Prophets is surely contained in this one saying.

NOTES

[1] New York, Harper, 1973, p. 106.
[2] London, Kegan Paul, 1905, ¶21, p. 72.
[3] September, 1976.
[4] *Animal Rights and Human Obligations,* Prentice-Hall, 1976.
[5] *The Next Two Hundred Years,* New York, Morrow, 1976.
[6] "Lo, the Poor Animals", *The Atlantic,* September, 1976, p. 59.
[7] Kahn, pp. 136-38.
[8] Cf. A. MacPherson, "Synthetic Food for Tomorrow's Billions", *Beyond Left and Right,* Morrow-Apollo, 1968, pp. 211-22.
[9] *The Complete Works of Tacitus,* M. Hadas, editor, Modern Library, 1942, pp. 659, 665.
[10] *The Rock Woman,* Selected Poems, Oxford, 1968, "Elegy at the Year's End", p. 22.

Part II

HOW WE FAIL

Chapter IV

ON THE MOST DANGEROUS VIRTUE

The Law and the Prophets, thus, teach that we are social animals and sons of bitches, that we should contain our dogs and not tear down our cathedrals. We are a funny lot and often delude ourselves. And one of the strange things about our insight into ourselves on the way to glory is that we are frequently the worst just when we assume we are doing quite all right. W.C. Field's friend "Doc" Atterbury, I think, well showed us that, while never giving a sucker an even break, we can be perfectly dignified in practising one-upmanship on our neighbour on English trains in which no smoking is permitted.

And so if I want to say something about the praise of fallen men, I will also want to reflect on their vices, on the way we all deceive ourselves, on our boredom which prevents us from enjoying what is to be enjoyed, on our hatreds which we are too often told lead us to the "new man". Let me begin here, then, with a passage from François Mauriac, with the paradox that sometimes even our virtues can operate pretty much like vices. Mauriac wrote: "But *sincerity* with regard to oneself is the virtue of our generation, so we should be bold and face up to our vices".[1]

Everybody knows, I think, that virtue is virtue and vice is vice. Not everybody, of course, is exactly sure which is which — and there is part of the rub. One much desired quality, however, seems almost universally admitted to be a virtue. This is *sincerity*. Doctrine will not save us, neither will works, nor faith alone but *sincerity* will. What God wants to know is not what we have done or what we have believed but rather whether we were authentic and honest and sincere with ourselves.

Nonetheless I have recently had occasion to wonder about this particular virtue. Inescapably almost, I have come to believe that, in the way it is used these days at least, sincerity is more probably a vice. But if it must be a virtue, certainly it is the most dangerous one about. To be sure, sincerity is not one of the prohibitions of the Law and the Prophets, nor of the Ten Commandments, nor is it one of the capital sins, neither is it one of the four moral virtues, nor yet one of the gifts of the Holy Spirit. Nevertheless, I have the impression that sincerity is rapidly becoming that very criterion by which all other values are judged.

But what is sincerity?

Yet when it comes right down to it, to find out anything at all substantial about sincerity is not easy. Just for curiosity, I spent one rainy Thursday afternoon searching our library for an adequate discussion of it. It turned out that the best discussions, and even these brief, were found in the Bible dictionaries. R.L. Scheef's discussion of the way sincerity is used in Scripture seemed the most typical:

> A quality of personal character or action which is free from falsification, deceit, or wickedness, and is characterized by purity, genuineness and the like. The various qualities associated with sincerity in the Bible are purity, genuineness, uprightness, truthfulness and godliness.
>
> The etymology of *eilikrineia* is uncertain. The idea behind the word, however, may have been that of being found true and pure when examined. This is expressed

in Paul's claim for sincerity "in the sight of God" (2 Cor 2:17).

. . . A distinctive meaning imparted to the idea of sincerity in the Bible is that of godliness or holiness. In 2 Cor 1:12, sincerity is mentioned in connection with holiness as being "godly sincerity". In this light, the "sincere mind" of 2 Pet 3:1 may be understood in the sense of a devout and godly mind aroused to true piety. Such sincerity is especially important for those who preach the Gospel.[2]

Sincerity in this tradition, of course, is clearly a noble virtue which seeks to bridge the gap between belief and conduct. It signifies a certain wholeness and consistency, a lack of foreign alloys, a purity of genuine uprightness. This is what the Latin word, *sincerus*, means. *The Oxford English Dictionary* shows that the word is used in the same way in English — freedom from duplicity, frankness, no mixture of disturbing elements.

Some problems

Since sincerity is obviously a necessary and good quality in this biblical and classical sense, what objection can there be to it? There is something subtle here. The trouble with sincerity was very simply stated by a colleague of mine, who pointed out that "Hitler was quite sincere". T.L. Jarman related something of this difficulty:

Hitler began clearly to form for himself his romantic sense of his mission to rebuild Germany — a romantic conception, but one he was to carry out with the greatest realism. In the midst of national disillusion and decay Hitler found for himself an objective to which he could devote all his energies. And not only could he create this sense of purpose for himself; he could give it to others. One of his early followers described his emotions on first hearing Hitler at a mass meeting in 1922:

"His words were like a scourge. When he spoke of the disgrace of Germany, I felt ready to spring on any enemy . . . glancing round, I saw that his magnetism was holding these thousands as one . . . I was a man of thirty-two, weary of disgust and disillusionment, a wanderer seeking a cause; a patriot without a channel for his patriotism, a yearner after the heroic without a hero. The intense will of the man, *the passion of his sincerity*, seemed to flow from him into me. I experienced an exaltation that could be likened only to religious conversion . . .".[8]

The problem is very clearly brought out here because Hitler was quite frank and clear and open. He really did state what he believed long ahead of his actions. Then, when he had a chance, he lived according to his beliefs. The irony is both that no one believed him and that many subsequently did. He was sincere.

This is, to be sure, the extreme case. To take another instance, at the University in California where I teach, there was a university-wide requirement that Catholic students must take a certain minimal number of hours of theological studies for graduation. The purpose of this provision was academic: that is, ignorance of religion is ignorance. Further, no one can possibly understand much of western and world civilization without some knowledge of Christianity. This requirement, whatever be its objective merit, produced rather striking results. One class of student immediately became "insincere" by declaring himself "non-Catholic" merely to escape the requirement. Others took the positive sincerity approach. That is, they maintained, God only wants us to believe what we think we can believe. Therefore there is no interest or necessity in discovering anything further about what we believe.

What is striking about this sort of formal "disbelief" today is, I think, that it is not usually embraced because of a belief in something else. At one time, we disbelieved in one religion or philosophy or science because we found

64

another more believable or convincing. This is no longer the case. Disbelief does not mean that some other truth is found. The justification for this new attitude is almost invariably based upon the notion of sincerity.

In Katherine Mansfield's short story, "The Daughters of the Late Colonel", the two spinster sisters are just coming to be aware of the social etiquette expected of them after their father's death:

Constantia had noticed nothing; she sighed.

"Do you think we ought to have our dressing gowns dyed as well?"

"Black?" almost shrieked Josephine.

"Well, what else?" said Constantia. "I was thinking — it doesn't seem quite sincere, in a way, to wear black out-of-doors and when we're fully dressed and then when we're at home . . ."[4]

Sincerity in this passage is exaggerated, of course, verging on hypocrisy almost, unable to distinguish between what is public and what is private. But it begins to suggest the difficulty I have with sincerity. For sincerity is concerned first with ourselves, with how *we* relate to ourselves. It is essentially in-going. That sincere persons are attractive, there is no doubt. Indeed, they may well be the most attractive of all. They have about them a certain inner serenity and genuineness. We all desire to be serene and whole and sincere. We are deeply affected when such quality is in others. And yet, sincerity and serenity always need a touch of vanity, a touch of how others see us, sometimes quite a big touch.

A complaisant indulgence for people's weaknesses

Lord Chesterfield wrote a letter to his son in 1747 entitled, "How to please". In a certain sense, I suspect, this letter might better have been entitled, "How to be insincere". "If you would particularly gain the affection and friendship of particular people, whether men or women", he advised, "Endeavour to find out their predominant excellency, if they have one, and their prevailing weakness, which everybody has; and do justice to the one, and something more than justice to the other".[5] Such flattery, of course, is not "sincere", for it does not tell what we really think or if it does, it is contrived. Yet, Lord Chesterfield was undoubtedly right. To be always and utterly sincere and frank is to forget what the world outside of ourselves is about.

Chesterfield went on, in a passage I quite like:

> Do not mistake me, and think that I mean to recommend to you abject and criminal flattery: no; flatter nobody's vices or crimes: on the contrary, abhor and discourage them. But there is no living in the world *without a complaisant indulgence for people's weaknesses,* and innocent though ridiculous vanities. If a man has a mind to be thought wiser, and a woman handsomer, than they really are, their error is a comfortable one to themselves, and an innocent one with regard to other people; and I would rather make them my friends by indulging them in it, than my enemies by endeavouring (and that to no purpose) to undeceive them.[6]

This is a kind of compassionate appreciation of our finiteness and our fallenness. We should for the most part let the errors that are "the comfortable ones" go. In other words, we are first to be considerate of others. We are not to be too surprised or scandalized by their weaknesses and faults. We cannot go about calling just every son of a bitch a son of a bitch! There must be a certain delicacy about our foibles. We need not wear black pyjamas nor destroy the small vanities of others on the grounds that we ought to be sincere with ourselves. We ought to leave our lovely cathedrals standing, even if they do betray a touch of vanity in the men who worship God in them.

Dom David Knowles once wrote several valuable and reflective essays on the changes in outlook during the past century. He believed that a new world began after World

War II which radically changed the traditional value system. A shift from emphasis on serving others to "a universal and overwhelming desire for personal realization" was the significant factor. The desire to discover who one was undermined any belief in an elite and eventually challenged all authority other than one's own personality.

This frame of mind, hostile to any way of life which in one way or another was guided by standards, values and "essences" outside the mind of the individual, was irked by constraint of any kind, whether of law or dogma. In the last analysis, existentialist and individualist thought is inconsistent with any intellectual acceptance of the universe as the work of an omnipotent and loving Creator, whose design and will can be known by his human creatures even without direct revelation, and in whose will, and there alone, is peace.[7]

When no intellectual connection is admittetd to be possible between the structure of the world and the centrality of the person and its desires, the person soon becomes its own value, not because it acknowledges something beyond itself, but because it declares itself to be itself. This is the very opposite of the essential note of personhood in classical Christian thought in which relatedness to others was the central aspect of the notion. There is no praise if there is only ourselves to praise.

A return to civility

Ferdinand Mount has traced the devastating effects of this change of viewpoint from a duty other oriented philosophy to a right self oriented one. He is most perceptive in emphasizing how the effects of sincerity or honesty have come to mean practically their contraries. For Mount, the virtue of civility is the one that contrasts most with sincerity.

Civility is that mode of behaviour which makes civilization possible. The features of this behaviour are:

courtesy and consideration towards both iudividuals and groups, opponents as well as allies; modesty, restraint, and moderation both in speech and action; obedience to established rules of procedure and conduct . . .

Civility demands that on frequent occasions your first loyalty is not to the unfettered expression of your own sensations, emotions and desires, but to other principles such as tolerance, respect, and even love of your neighbour. On the calculus of civility, it may be your duty to pretend a sympathy you do not feel, to hold back, to refrain from saying or doing all that you would like to do, to say and do things that you would not have done left to yourself, in general to settle for half a loaf rather than all or nothing.

For those who regard *sincerity* as the supreme good, this is the supreme blasphemy. The profession of what you do not believe is hypocrisy, the sin against the light. The suppression of the pure impulse is rank unauthenticity, the acceptance of the mark of the bourgeoisie.[8]

Thus, sincerity easily becomes, in reality, a vice, a way to trample on the sensibilities and foibles of others because we do not want to appear other than the way we actually feel. There is something mad about this result, something that makes us realize the twistings of our fallenness, something that encloses us completely within our own world.

Sincerity, then, is undoubtedly a virtue, indeed, a very important and powerful virtue, as Paul said. But it is a most dangerous virtue, for it has no content itself. We can be sincere about almost anything. The question must first always be: about what is it that we are sincere? When sincerity becomes its own norm, it is the most selfish and individualistic of theories. We cannot always "tell it just like it is", nor emote "just how we feel". Our feelings, as important as they are, are just not that reliable. Furthermore, there are times, many times, when we must give up our "right" to how we feel.

The Christian ethic, then, is not found upon ourselves but on others, others who are by no means perfect. We should indeed practice what we preach. But *what* it is we preach is all important. There are quite a few people who ought not to practice their preachments, because what they preach is awful. Sincerity, consequently, can become a very subtle substitute for any need to consider the world outside of ourselves, its realities, its weaknesses and its structures. "We are saved if we are sincere . . .". But it all depends. The ultimate vice is that which substitutes oneself for the cause and order of all things. In our time, I suspect, pride seems to manifest itself as sincerity. We no longer need to believe anything nor even do anything. We need not study anything nor reflect on anything. We need merely to be whole and guileless, genuine, frank, upright, and, yes, sincere.

In such a world, however, we have not only eliminated the Cross and sacrifice, but we have even removed the need to have anything but ourselves — a rather boring result to which I shall next turn. It is no accident that the refusal to study the drama of existence or revelation on the grounds of sincerity should lead to nothing else. The only thing left when we are sincere with ourselves is ourselves. We are left with boredom and talk ourselves into believing it is the greatest of virtues.

Lord Chesterfield had a healthier instinct. He was more correct and even more Christian, for somewhere along the line we should learn to please others for no other reason than it is the nice thing to do for them. *And there is no living in the world without a complaisant indulgence for people's weaknesses.* Civility begins in etiquette and politeness, with not encouraging your Great Dane to jump on crotchety gentlemen's laps. It is no wonder then that sincerity can destroy the very basis of culture. For it attacks the very heart of the belief upon which our civilization is built — that respect for even the littlest ones is the first law. It is towards this and not towards ourselves

69

that sincerity must be directed even though we are indeed persons and so made from creation.

NOTES

[1] *God and Mammon*, 1936.
[2] *Interpreter's Dictionary of the Bible*, V. 4, p. 377.
[3] *The Rise and Fall of Nazi Germany*, Signet, 1961, p. 97. Italics added.
[4] *Selected Stories*, Oxford, 1969, p. 253.
[5] In *Selected English and American Essays*, Holt, 1957, pp. 19-20.
[6] *Ibid.*, p. 21.
[7] "This Century of Change, The Moral Background", *The Tablet*, London, 15 December 1973, pp. 1197-98.
[8] "The Recovery of Civility", *Encounter*, London, 2 July 1973, pp. 31, 41.

Chapter V

ON BOREDOM

Too much sincerity, then, can leave us with an overdose of ourselves. Chesterton said somewhere that there is no such thing as an uninteresting thing, only uninterested persons. The result may be what one of my friends calls "boring", the worst invective imaginable. And being bored has something to do with our perception of how the world is and where it is going. Today, evidence abounds on all sides that the melioristic beliefs dominant in the great culture at least since the Enlightenment are at an end. Let me cite just one example as it comes from such an unexpected source: "Marlon Brando's methodological search (for his home on Tahiti) was based on the grimmest of calculations: 'I'm convinced the world is doomed. The end is near. I want a place where my family and I can be self-sufficient and survive' ".[1] The grimness and the melancholy do weigh heavily. It is difficult for me not to wonder why.

Gradually at first, more recently like a tide, it has become almost socially fashionable to profess a loss of hope in any this-worldly future. A lady in a *New Yorker* cartoon is at breakfast in the city with her sombre husband poring angrily over the newspaper. She says to him: "What's disgusting today, dear?"[2] This at least catches the humour of it. Until yesterday, the future was used as an instrument to reject Christian notions of sin and evil.

Christianity was once attacked for being against progress. Now it is more likely to be criticised for being for it, for *not* being disgusted at everything today. Christianity is accused of failing to preserve a sense of sin in our culture and a reasonable judgment about what we can expect of man. Many are beginning to take the Fall in a hopeless sense. Whence comes the insistent demand that men and the world be "transformed" somehow by psychological or sociological or genetic means so that *evil* will be removed. So the great hopes of post-World War II are failing. Europe will not unite. The Third World appears to lapse more and more into a series of petty despotisms. The marxist world has produced only Gulag with its Eastern European equivalents. Malcolm Muggeridge wonders if we are not heading for a new dark age. There is a sense of ennui, of fate.

Tedium and social heresies

And there is cause for pessimism. But what is perhaps new today, I think, is that our pessimism is rooted in a spiritual cause. It is not a pessimism resulting from an earthquake or a tidal wave, though, currently, even such natural disasters as pestilence, earthquake, fire, sharks and plagues have become common in the popular media. Rather there is a spiritual tiredness, a tedium, a sadness that has lost not only hope for discovering the good, but has a positive distaste for the good as defined by classical Christianity. Escapism, self-interest, perversion, all ever parts of human reality to some degree, are rife among those who sense future political and ecological doom. Evil is no longer a spiritual abstraction or something individuals do, but is discovered in concrete movements and attitudes of ordinary men in their public lives.

This sense of despair in our contemporary culture deserves more attention than it has been receiving, for it is of a peculiar nature. There is a growing suspicion that all the revolutions in which we have placed our sequential hopes are failing us. Few wish to acknowledge this because it implies a questioning of the very premise that "men can make men happy", the premise upon which the modern world was largely based. Classical Christianity had taught that men could *not* make themselves happy, of course, and was rejected by the modern mind for this reason. What we now see is the rejection of this rejection, as it were, which results not in a return to Christianity so much as a dryness of spiritual energy which sees no place further to go.

We are not unaware of similar crises in past civilizations that found themselves in great difficulties. The Roman civilization in its decline has become something of a paradigm. But the contemporary crisis is more serious in that Christianity itself forms part of the culture. The dominant ideology appears not as "orthodoxy" but as "heresy", which occurs in sociological guise. We have Manicheanism, Donatism, and Pelagianism, along with Millennarism, Montanism, Arianism, and Gnosticism. But these appear in political forms which we fail to realize. We are beginning to get Jansenism, Quietism, and even Averroism. Christianity does not appear as something fresh but as something old and outmoded. The lukewarm and the lax are taken as its representatives, while believers in the central line of orthodoxy are judged to be fanatics. And indeed, they are so, in a way, when they are compared to the prevailing standards of contemporary moral practice and truth.

Most of Christianity's innovations of charity, health care and education are rapidly falling into the hands of the state and the unions, which bureaucratize their spirit and life, which know only "justice" in their manner of acting. Sacrifice and kindness, extra effort and diversity of talent become threats to unions and professions and interest groups. We confuse envy with equality. We look upon generosity and innovation as exploitation. We allow no one to have more or to do more.

We seek, then, to make our collectivity substitute for our free acts wherein our persons are truly formed. We are bored and tired so that we no longer have the energy to conceive alternatives. We are unfair to past generations from whom we refuse to learn. We insist on beginning all things anew, as if we had no duties towards our past. We have even lost our confidence that we can know the truth from the error so we are helpless before ideologies which speak confidently but which destroy and distort human life and freedom, truth and virtue. We know our universities are largely controlled by vested ideologies, yet we hesitate to mention it.

We refuse, further, to be guided in our private lives by what is good, even though we long for, insist on, a kind of public morality which no evidence gives us reason to suspect can actually come about at this level. We have come to tolerate as "human rights" those very vices Paul listed in *Romans* and in *Corinthians*. Moreover, we are advised that the virtuous life — responsible marriage, children, household, zeal, innovation — are causes of our corporate doom. We have, without recognizing it, turned the whole anti-Manichean polemic of the early Church around. The natural things have become the evils, as the Manicheans originally maintained, the unnatural vices have come to be called "good", since they do not result in begetting more of our own kind.

How is it that the classical virtues in which we are supposed to have rejoiced have become the objects of disgust and depression? How is it possible that the worldly enterprise of today has come to be conceived in terms of pessimism and tedium? Initially, we cannot ever forget the centrality of the Christian notion of freedom. It is really true that men *can* reject the good — even hate it, as I shall suggest in the next chapter. Indeed, such is the crucial drama behind all political and economic forces into which our contemporary discussions of good and evil have been cast. We refuse to consider *personal* destiny, morality and conduct unless they be translated into social or collective realities. No holiness is allowed unless it falls within a social, ideological framework of progress for one school or conservation for another, but both in this world. And it is this that grounds our pessimism and despair, since we find it impossible to establish our ultimate destiny upon the welfare of some part of the human race that chances to be born after we are.

The despair of optimism in the West

Laszek Kolakowski has carefully emphasized the danger within Christianity of denying its own position with regard to permanence of evil.

> In Christian thought, the damnation of the devil and the concept of original sin are most precise forms which clothe the negation of the contingent character of evil. I think that that negation is of extreme importance for our own culture, but that we can also discern in the Christian world a strong temptation to abandon that position to rally itself about the optimistic tradition of the Enlightenment which believes in the final reconciliation of all that is into one final, universal harmony.
>
> The two complementary ideas are at the very heart of Christian culture — namely, that humanity has been fundamentally saved by the coming of Christ and that, since man has been chased from an earthly paradise, every human being is fundamentally condemned if we consider him in his natural state, without the aid of grace — these must only be considered together in order to avoid a haughty optimism or a despair which would follow the consideration of the two ideas independently one from another.[3]

Precisely the reinvigoration of the idea of original sin and the permanence of evil are required to save the social order itself which stands torn between Marxist optimism and ecological pessimism in a way that causes both to reject central elements in the human person — its freedom in the case of Marxism, its goodness in the case of ecology.

When we do not attend to the centrality of original sin and the reality of evil, then these doctrines resurface in forms that attack something more basic, the person himself. Original sin reappears in a secular form in Marxism's fantastic belief that the root of evil lies in property division. Original sin rises again in ecology's view that men's normal drives will destroy them. It is founded in some strands of psychology, in man's incapacity to know what he is. R.D. Laing wrote:

> Millions of people have died in this century and millions more are going to . . . because we cannot break this knot. It seems a comparatively simple knot, but it is tied very, very tight — round the throat, as it were, of the whole human species. But don't believe me because I say so, look in the mirror and see for yourself.[4]

It is precisely this concentration on our "species" that bothers and confuses us, because what exists are persons. The species man will not be saved.

The common element that constantly reappears, then, in all modern social heresies, that is, the locus in which takes place the contact between God and man, is that proposition which sees the well-being of *humanity* as the criterion for politics and judgments about persons. But persons in classical Christian thought were rather considered the true basis for both social thought and spirituality, and not some second level abstraction like "humanity". What has become the final justification of most contemporary discussions, both pessimistic and optimistic versions, is this continuance-in-being for the "species", since this is the only worldly good that seems to transcend space and time.[5]

Individual and corporate survival

Christianity has generally looked upon God and the world from the viewpoint of the individual person. In the

City of God and in the City of Babylon, Augustine never confused abstract collectivities with societies based upon actual personal wills and beings even when these societies did transcend in their vision the present temporal order. The spiritual life and destiny of mankind were, thus, not conceived after the manner of an abstract group or logical construct, but after the destiny of the persons with names around whom all social and economic life were seen to evolve. In this sense, the "institutions" that survive the individual life of men which bear their reality — states, empires, corporations, bureaus, schools, dioceses, families, religious orders — were not conceived to be the locus of salvation. While these did often last beyond the life of a given person, or several generations of persons, they too are ephemeral. They belong to the things that also pass away. The temporal sequence of very few collectivities stretches for more than two or three hundred years in an unbroken line. Some universities like Oxford and Cambridge go back centuries; the English monarchy is very old; the organizational structure of the Catholic Church is unique in being so venerable. Very few of the one hundred and fifty odd political states of the world can claim continuous governmental forms for more than a hundred years, even though certain popular attitudes, beliefs and customs may seem almost ageless.

However the notion that some institutional arrangement, be it of a small group, a political state, or the whole world, can substitute for the destiny embodied in each individual person is the form under which ultimate beatitude is presented most often today. The "survival" of mankind comes to be substituted for the reality within which man actually lives. And when this "survival" is conceived in terms which undermine the person's very mode of earthly being on the grounds that such is necessary for a future generation, we are left with a kind of despair and pessimism which identifies doom with any so-called threat to survival.

This too neatly avoids personal reflection or comprehension about a destiny that is not restricted to the abstract terms of an on-going collectivity which has no "existence" except at the notional level. The only possible "existence" of the collectivity of all the human persons who in fact have ever existed — perhaps 85-95 billions — can only be grounded in the Augustinian sense of the City of God. And that existence is premised not upon "survival" of future generations but on the quality of the spiritual choices of persons within the context of their histories and lives that will normally and necessarily be lived in very imperfect states and human conditions.

Dante was said to have dreamed of a society of the world in which all the potentialities of human ' existence were actualized. Yet it is clear that most of the potentialities of most men who have so far lived were not actualized. Indeed, the proposition that life leaves no potentiality unactualized is probably a denial of choice and freedom. When we choose one life, we reject another we might very well have lived. We can expect the potentialities for both good and evil to find further embodiment in future ages. But any notion of a "human survival" in finite time seen not in terms of Augustine's personal choice and destiny within God's saving grace must end up in a kind of subtle revival of Latin Averroism, which felt there was only one intellect and individual persons were merely instances of it.

Christianity rightly rejected this notion which, I feel, can often be sensed in recent scholarly treatments of survival ethics, either in nuclear warfare discussions or in ecological ones. The rejection of the "two truths" implied in medieval Averroism was precisely to connect existing human persons to the structure of the world and to God through it and through his call in it. Persons really do have their autonomy, their freedom, precisely in this world, in this history, no matter what its secular form. We miss the intellectual depth of the current controversies, I feel, if we fail to see this more profound issue.

But the separation of any personal destiny beyond the collective abstraction in which "mankind" is said to have existence from that of a personal immortality leaves the actual individual with a kind of hopeless hope.[6] What does it really mean to sacrifice one generation for another? How do we know that one generation of men, whenever they live, is happier than another? We know that the sun will eventually fail us. Our kind, some of it, may succeed in reaching other planets in other solar systems. But eventually we shall fail on the planet Earth. How much difference it makes theologically whether we survive as a race for another few million years or not is by no means clear. What is important, from the Christian viewpoint, is *how* we survive.

On being tired

Darwinism was held to be a belief in the survival of the fittest. And social Darwinism has made the most ruthless of virtues the means of fitting. Some social compact theories have maintained that the whole of the weak ganged up on the strong to survive, while Nietzsche seemed to have felt that Christianity's doctrine of meekness and love of enemies (a point I shall return to in a later chapter) definitely propagated an inferior type of human. So we must have a criterion of survival other than survival itself. But the history of the human race ought not to be a gigantic replay of, say, *The Ten Little Indians,* in which only the cleverest manage to stay on. Indeed, Christianity, while not rejecting the primacy of life and being, has ever taught that there were values higher than physical survival for the individual and for the race. To a greater extent than we care to acknowledge, the boredom and pessimism of our era are rooted, not merely in the sense of natural or man-made doom that is so strikingly present, but in the alternatives in either a successful Marxism or in ecology which would promise us nothing but a stagnant repetition of what went before. Their removal of "evil" could only result in the utmost dullness. It would destroy any praise within our fallenness.

We are not used to admitting the possibility of the

good being freely rejected in any or all of its varieties and forms. Evil, tradition held, is to be chosen under some aspect of the good or else it would not be at all attractive. We are not Manichees who give evil a substantial counter deity who created the material world in his image. Yet the good could be positively rejected by men. Men can reject and regret the kind of world that God gave to them.[7]

Sadness, tiredness before a conquering idea is perhaps a normal reaction. Gualberto Gismondi, a religious apologist of Marxism, recently wrote: "Atheism today is at the centre of Christian attention since it assumes the form of scandal, stimulus and challenge. Far from accusing it of tiredness, it presents itself as vital and vigorous . . .".[8] By direct contrast, and with considerably more empirical experience of the alternative, Alexander Solzhenitsyn told the American labour leaders in a graphic passage:

> I understand, I sense that you're tired. You're fatigued, but you have not yet really suffered the terrible trials of the twentieth century which have rained down on the old continent. You're tired, but not as tired as we are, lying crushed to the ground for sixty years. You're tired, but the communists who want to destroy your system aren't tired; they aren't tired at all.[9]

One of the classical mysteries of human history lies in these passages — why are the children of light so much less energetic? Why is it that men can be so confused about the good? Why is it that enthusiasm for movements that distort men do find such adherence and enthusiasm?

Charity is said to rejoice in the divine good. Yet there was a kind of sadness that resulted from this same good.[10] Man can, in fact, be sad, tired, depressed because of the order of good and redemption he finds himself in. Thus a kind of sadness may be less than the direct hatred of God because He is God. But it interprets all the effects of God as regrettable, dejecting, unworthy of man.[11] These spiritual roots of public problems are often neglected, since we concentrate too much on institutions and even ideas. Christianity refuses to neglect the personal status of each man. Likewise it insists that institutions, states, collectivities are made up of persons. These social environments can indeed be such that we are cut off from much that is good. We often must go against much of our culture or milieu to see and accept what we believe to be good. Scripture tells us that the children of this world are wiser than those of the Kingdom. It talks about the salt becoming tasteless, even though we are to be the salt of the earth. There is, too, a certain sense of the spiritual tedium here that is endemic to the human condition, one that overvalues the enterprises of the world, one that finds the salt of truth and life tasteless.

On not being satisfied with too little

Boredom and sadness, however, are to be carefully distinguished from a series of ideas and conditions at first easily confused with them. Leisure, idleness, recreation, play, amusement — those concepts Aristotle laid so much stress on in the Eighth Book of the *Politics* — may look at first sight like boredom or sadness.[12] Play I shall talk about more in a later discussion. And amusement is to restore and delight us. Recreation enables us to return to work. Idleness is that unconcern that allows us time and space for reflection and refreshment, while leisure is the end of work, that big part of life beyond necessity. The promise of all human and worldly things, then, carries them beyond themselves. The world is also *Word* with its own consistency and intelligibility destined to illuminate, satisfy us to a greater extent than we can really comprehend.

Yet there is nothing in the world of man or nature that can ultimately calm us. We live in a time in which new and fresh ideas are rapidly exhausted, not just because there are now so many of us reflecting on what we are given in so many different ways and languages, but mostly because we are not designed to be satisfied by so little. And yet this boredom is not yet that deeper spiritual sadness which not merely realizes that truth and goodness are not exhausted by what is in fact true and good in its own way, but is even dejected that the good and true and even the beautiful should be the way they are. This is the border and beginning of pride, which would like to create its own world because it cannot conceive that the given, redeemed one is really a better one, albeit a fallen one in many ways.

Once arrived at this point then, spiritual tedium and moroseness easily slip into hatred, into an active, relentless rejection of the good because it is good. The sober melancholy, the doom which we find so often and ever more frequently in our time has, I think, roots rather of this spiritual nature. It is defined not so much by the limits of growth or of nature, nor by the finiteness of man, but by the choices we allow ourselves to make, choices which lie at the basis of what it is to be free. Such choices can allow us to be bored with what is true, depressed at what is indeed of God.

Nonetheless, to conclude, if we can choose damnation we can also choose light even in our fallibility. Such are the choices which allow us the ultimate freedom, that of responding to the discovery for ourselves, in the fabric and history of our own personal lives and loves, in whatever generation, place, or era we àre, that we are first loved. Ultimately there is no boredom if we choose the good. And so boredom is being an uninterested person who cannot see the glory of things because he chooses not to do so. And from boredom it is but a short step to hatred, a step we shall next consider.

NOTES

[1] *Time*, 24 May 1976.
[2] Whitney Darrow, *The New Yorker*, 23 September 1974, p. 31.

[3] L. Kolakowski, "Il diable, peut-il être sauvé?", *Contrepoint*, Paris, ¶20, 1976, pp. 130-31.

[4] *The Politics of the Family*, Toronto, Canadian Broadcasting Company, 1969, p. 49.

[5] Cf. E. Benoit, "First Steps to Survival", *The Bulletin of the Atomic Scientists*, March, 1976, p. 42.

[6] Probably the best statement of a natural religion which has no supernatural propositions or beliefs for ethical life is still John Stuart Mill's *Nature and Utility of Religion*, New York, Liberal Arts, 1958.

[7] Cf. J.V. Schall, "Some Remarks on the Current Problematic of Theoretic Atheism", *Homiletic and Pastoral Review*, October, 1972.

[8] Cf. S. Fiorelli, "Il Marxismo e il rapporto tra Democrazia e Socialismo", *IDOC*, Marzo-Aprile, 1976, p. 77.

[9] Speech of 9 July 1975, *Free Trade Union News*, July-August, 1975, p. 30.

[10] Cf. Aquinas, II-II, 35, 2.

[11] Cf. Aquinas, II-II, 34, 1 and 2.

[12] Cf. J.V. Schall, *Far Too Easily Pleased: A Theology of Play, Contemplation, and Festivity*, Los Angeles, Benzinger, 1976.

Chapter VI

ON HATRED

From the temptation of not wanting the good to be good, it is easy, as I hinted, to become much more active, violent, disturbed about the good. We are in a world in which men hate and insist it is a virtue. In a recent audience after some wild disturbances in Rome, Paul VI reminded us, "Hatred is not civilized".[1] And Paul said to Titus, "For we ourselves were once foolish, disobedient, led astray, slaves to various passions, passing our days in malice and envy, *hated by men and hating one another*" (3:3). And Pascal bluntly stated in his *Pensées*, "All men naturally hate one another" (451). What are we to make of hatred, especially when we are often told we must praise it?

The New Testament is a book grounded in love, generosity, forgiveness. In it we find the First Great Commandment, along with the Second, the fulfilment of the Law and the Prophets. Yet on actually reading and re-reading what are often the most solemn parts of Scripture, how often must we be struck by the frequency with which both the Old and New Testaments deal with hatred? In Matthew's Sermon on the Mount, for example, we read, "You have heard how it was said, 'You must love your neighbour and hate your enemy' . . ." (5:43). In Luke, this passage becomes, "Love your enemies, do good to those who hate you", almost as if we can expect that there will always be those who will hate us (6:27). Earlier in Luke, we are astonished to hear, "Happy are you when people hate you, drive you out, abuse you . . ." (6:22). Surely we do not find it too easy to be happy about such things.

In *Wisdom,* Yahweh loves all that exists and holds "nothing of what you have made in abhorrence, for had you hated anything, you would not have formed it" (11:25). Yet Yahweh turns out to hate quite a few things. "You hate all evil men, liars you destroy; murderers and frauds Yahweh detests" (Ps 5:5-6). Zechariah informs us, "These are the things you must do. Speak the truth to each other, let the judgment at your gates be such as conduces to peace; do not secretly plot evil against one another; do not love false oaths; since all of this is what I hate. It is Yahweh who speaks" (8:16-17). And in *Proverbs,* "There are six things that Yahweh hates, seven that his soul abhors; a haughty look, a lying tongue, hands that shed innocent blood, a heart that weaves wicked plots, feet that hurry to do evil, a false witness who lies with every breath, a man who sows dissention among his brothers" (6:16-19). So while creation is loved by Yahweh, much of what men do to themselves and one another is given the graphic stigma of "hatred". Men can, evidently, cause even Yahweh to hate.

In *Job,* we find a theme that takes us to John. "Others of them hate the light, know nothing of its ways, avoid its paths" (24:13). John in his own spirit continues, "And indeed, everybody who does wrong hates the light and avoids it, for fear his actions shall be exposed . . ." (3:20). And John's warnings become more sombre, frightening even: "If the world hates you, remember that it hated me before you. If you belonged to the world, the world would love you as its own, but because you do not belong to the world, because my choice withdrew you from the world, therefore the world hates you" (15:18). Again during the Last Supper, there is even cited the highly disturbing warning from Psalm 35, "They hated me for no reason".

Matthew had, indeed, earlier attested to the cause of this unexpected paradox surging about the revelation of divine love. "You will be hated by all men on account of my name" (10:22). This seems to be something more than moroseness or boredom that the good is good. Rather, this suggests that when we are hated because of our discipleship, something more is taking place than just an attitude towards ourselves. John's First Epistle admonished that "You must not be surprised, brothers, when the world hates you" (3:12-13). Yet I at least confess that most of us are deeply surprised that this should be so. Paul, to be sure, told Titus that he was hated by men and hated them in return (3:3). And this was so that men could recognize the share of hatred they bear in themselves. The history of Christianity, in any case, has not shown that the expectation of these realistic predictions about hatred were wrong or would not be a fundamental part of the world in which any generation found itself.

And what is hatred?

Hatred, at first sight, seems to be an easy thing to define and condemn, even though from Scriptures we must be already aware that there seems to be some mystery about it. Few are unaware that the world is full of social hatred — nationalistic, racial, tribal, economic, ethnic, sexual and religious — as well as personal ones, rooted in individual lives and controversies. Hatred contains a strong dose of will in it. Hatred is not just "dislike" or "distaste", but includes a positive decision that bears upon the very humanity of what is hated as well as of him who hates. Hatred is something of the spiritual order that bears upon ultimate values.

Our very hatred implies an intrinsic recognition of free choice somewhere in what is hated, some fundamental criticism that what is hated ought to be otherwise. Thus we cannot accurately speak of "hating" earthquakes, snakes, freezing winds, or baroque architecture. Whether we can hate "institutions", like the Internal Revenue Bureau or the House of Commons, is a question to which we will have to return as it is the origin of much really violent contemporary hatred. Hatred, finally, has its object in something spiritual and human, at least intelligent.

Discussing hatred, nevertheless, would be much easier were there not things we really ought to hate. Hatred is in fact the proper response to what is evil.[1] To love absolutely everything indiscriminately, no matter what its nature or condition, is a vice. Loving all things can in this sense reveal a certain naïvté which easily ends up by approving things that are quite harmful. This is why there are "six things that Yahweh hates, seven that his soul abhors". There is a famous passage in Machiavelli's *Prince* that coolly, calculatingly emphasizes the problem:

> Whence it may be seen that hatred is gained as much by good works as by evil, and therefore, as I said before, a prince who wishes to maintain the state is often forced to do evil, for when a party, whether populace, soldiery, or nobles . . . is corrupt, you must follow its humour and satisfy it, and in that case good works will be inimical to you (C. 19).

This passage is, to be sure, blatant since it cynically looks upon both *good* and *evil* as tools to be used for power. Furthermore, it makes it quite clear that a whole people may themselves be corrupt at a given time, something we are often reluctant to admit even though there is considerable evidence for its possibility and actuality in history.

Hatred of the Poor = *Hatred of the good.*

Machiavelli also recognized something very ominously true which the characters of, say, Iago in Shakespeare or Billy Budd in Melville seem to recall, namely, that the good — good works or good people — do not automatically produce love and affection in those who behold or receive them. We have a very short-sighted view of human nature, consequently, if we think that the sole cause of hatred is evil. The New Testament, as I have indicated, more frequently suggests the opposite. Hatred is often the response to Christ. Psalm 69 had also grieved, "More people hate me for no reason than I have hairs on my head". While we read in *Lamentations*, "They hunted me, harried me like a bird, they who hate me for no reason" (3:52). There is this constant theme that hatred has "no reason", almost as if hatred had no cause, a response to that "absence of good" which the philosophers indicate as evil.

C.S. Lewis often pointed out that there seems to be greater hatred when there is greater love and sacrifice and goodness — almost as if goodness itself could perhaps be the missing cause for hatred. And this necessarily brings us to Augustine through Matthew: "No man can be the slave of two masters: he will either hate the first and love the second, or treat the first with respect and the second with scorn. You cannot be the slave of both God and money" (Mt 6:24). What then divides and unites men ultimately? Ever since Augustine, the Christian answer to this question has taken on a peculiar quality of its own, a quality that is directly pertinent to the widespread hatred that is so often present today, that hatred which is directed against groups, classes and peoples and is justified by some corporate guilt theory expressed in political or economic ideology, itself justified by the mystical claim of being in a better "future". We are united and divided in Augustine not by our religion (the City of God is not co-terminous with the Church), nor by our race, nor by our nationality, nor by our sex, nor by our language, nor by our class. What unites and divides us cannot be placed in a cause extrinsic to us, in something we either are through no choice of our own or through some accident of our background.

We are, then, divided by what we love and, consequently, by what we hate. "What we see, then, is that two societies have issued from two kinds of love. Worldly society has flowered from selfish love which dared to despise even God, whereas the communion of saints is rooted in a love that is ready to trample on the self". This comes from Paul's notion that there is only Christ, no distinction in his followers (Col 3:10-11; Eph 4:13; Gal 3:27-28). The second city is built precisely from hatred towards the first wherever it is found. And it is only found where there are persons who do God's will.

If it is true then, that we are to hate what is evil in ourselves and in others, still we must account somehow for the kind of metaphysical hatred that exists in the world and which is directed precisely against the good because it is good. No one who beholds the vision of God could not love him, as Scripture teaches. But what we can hate in God are his punishments and his forbidding certain actions by divine law.[4] The Pharisees in the New Testament were told that they would have had no sin had not Christ come. That is, it is quite possible to hate the precise way God chose to save us.

Evil cannot bear the good

This line of thought leads me to the questions, difficult to pose, but still real enough in implication: Does one hate God by hating his image in man? And here, I mean God's image in precisely the kind of human being that we find in history and Scripture. We have seen that Scripture speaks of Yahweh hating men when they violate his commands. But this is something that is based precisely upon God's maintaining the kind of being he created.[5] Part of loving the good *is* hating the evil. And there is no compromise with this. Forgiving evil does not mean ignoring it or calling it good. "Good, as it ripens, becomes continually more different not only from evil but from good", C.S. Lewis wrote in *The Great Divorce*. "I do not think that all who choose the wrong road perish; but their rescue consists in being put back on the right road . . . Evil can be undone, but it cannot 'develop' into good".[6] So there is no escape, not only from the need to hate evil but from the knowledge of what precisely it is.

Undoubtedly one of the most startling aspects of the revival of Christianity in Russia is precisely this explicit recognition of the reality of evil and hatred as it touches the human person. Solzhenitsyn said on June 30, 1975:

> It is almost a joke now in the Western World, in the twentieth century, to use words like "good" and "evil". They have become almost old-fashioned concepts, but they are very real and genuine concepts. These are concepts from a sphere which is higher than us — good and evil. And instead of getting involved in base, petty, short-sighted political calculations and games we have to recognize that the concentration of world evil and the tremendous *force of hatred* is there and is flowing from there throughout the world. And we have to stand up against it and not hasten to give to it, give to it, give to it, everything that it wants to swallow.

There is here again this uncompromising recognition that there is in fact hatred and that it is an active force in the world. This widespread hatred for existing men is rooted in, and usually justified by, an ideology that depersonalizes men and especially women. The root cause is a belief in the "necessity" of history and its evolution along a predetermined pattern which enables us to destroy classes or types of people presumed to be the cause of evils. The authentic reaction to this kind of thinking is precisely rediscovering the fact that the world is made up of human beings, fallen persons who choose and act.

The locus of evil and good is always this human will which cannot escape to some abstraction to justify what it does against men. This is why the Russian dissidents insist upon documenting and identifying every person who is persecuted and every one who does the persecuting, how orders are signed and carried out, who did precisely what.

Here there is an absolute rejection of any excuse or subterfuge that would blame the evils on some idea or other intellectual rationalization that has no substance. Men who fail to see men are ever the ones in whom irresponsibility is found. There is a deep recognition here of the ultimate value and dignity of the human being and in the freedom of his will.

Whoever destroys the human body also attacks God

A further dimension of this hatred for God in man, it seems to me, can be seen in a remark of Kuehnelt-Leddihn:

> . . . Man has been created in the image of God, which means not only that God in a certain sense is anthromorphic, but also — which is equally important — that man is theomorphic. Thus whoever assails the image of man in an all-out radical way, whoever is anti-Humanist (taking the term in its classical connotation), whoever distorts, denigrates, perverts, disfigures and vilifies the human body also attacks God indirectly and sides with the forces of darkness, with Satan himself.[6]

And no doubt it is true, the human person in the concrete structure and destiny he has actually been given is what is more and more being *hated*. If we read much of the biological, ecological, psychological and sociological literature today, there is little question that it is the *kind* of men and women we are that is believed to be the cause of our ills.[7] Some "ideal" of what men ought to be has come to be used against the actual neighbours who do exist.

Not only, then, do men refuse to accept the supernatural destiny of each person who bears a name, which is implicit in the rejection of a Marxist or other utopian view of a paradise on Earth achieved by the sacrifice of one or another generation, but there is more and more a hatred of precisely the moral and ethical norms required to live a goodly life in this world, the kind we find recommended in Paul, for example. Scientists are even beginning to propose changing the very genetic structure of man in order to allow us to bypass the norms and restrictions that are placed upon us in our present fallen, finite, but redeemed status in which any real progress ultimately depends also on grace.

With Marxism and political utopianism of most sorts, however, the object of hatred is still generally men in their corporate existence. Some group or class is charged with *causing* the evil in the world such that its elimination will bring bliss and happiness. With much of the more recent scientific approaches or sociological ones, it is formally the historical, concrete person who is born of woman into the world as a child that is hated. Population theorists are telling us that our natural structures and normal tendencies and desires are what is wrong. They tell us we cannot save ourselves by our wills and by our intelligence exercised according to the being we now are.

Not only do the long lists of faults and failures and deformities listed by Paul in *Romans*, then, find positive advocates in our time as expressions of our so-called "natural rights", but we have come to hate the kind of persons who would dare to define any such things to be evil. More often than we care to admit, we are not permitted by public opinion to call, say, abortion an evil or suggest that homosexuality has anything in the slightest wrong with it. At a private level, anything men might "do" is coming to be seen as an expression of "human dignity", no matter what it might be. And thus when we come to maintain that what "ought" to be done or not done is itself a divine thing ultimately, that the kind of being given to the human person is a gift, a form which he did not create himself, we see how it is possible that this finite person himself may come to be hated and through him the cause of his being created the way he is.

Christianity insists, then, in locating responsibility for evil and hate in the disorder of the human will and not in some extrinsic movement, biological mistructure or evolutionary miscalculation. Christian tradition has always recognized that men can turn away from God because they do not want to be subject to his rule.[8] This has been called pride, the worst and first of sins. God could in fact be hated when men felt themselves to be the makers of their own ultimate laws, of their own personhood.[9] This hatred was always and necessarily seen through the nature and revelation that God gave to men. But what was ultimately rejected was God who gave such a creation to us. Boredom with the good and pride in the self, then, can lead to a positive hatred for God in the *way* his goodness is manifested and revealed.

Real hands, real faces, real persons

What is of value in the universe, then, centres about the personhood of man in so far as this is a gift of God. Hatred of God can only directly be expressed through hatred of the kind of being and law man is given for his own ultimate happiness, which is never anything less than God himself in his triune life. And thus it is possible, indeed, likely, that the greatest hatred of God will be meted out on innocent, good men. The innocence of the Man on the Cross is more than symbolic in this sense. This too is probably why the child is so often the ultimate victim of real hatred of God, since the child has, as such, no other protection but God's laws in the hearts of men and women. "If the world hates you, remember that it hated me before you . . .". It is in this context that the Gospel words about children have come to have a new meaning today. "Anyone who welcomes this little child in my name welcomes me; and anyone who welcomes me welcomes the one who sent me" (Lk 9:48). Again, the Christian view allows for no abstractions when dealing with persons who are the images of God.

When we see the faces and hands of our children and our brothers — their real faces and their real hands —

93

we begin to see God too. "Anyone who claims to be in the light but hates his own brothers is still in the dark" (1 Jn 2:8). ". . . . A man who does not love his brother that he can see cannot love God whom he has never seen . . . " (1 Jn 4:20). The context in which these passages are of supreme importance is that of the dehumanizing movements, practices and ideas of our times which concentrate on the very being and personhood of men as the object of their hatreds. When this hatred bears directly on the free expression of the person in the totalitarian system (here Solzhenitsyn's powerful chapters in *The Gulag Archipelago* are perhaps the most important witness against this) on man's physical or sexual being, on his right to be "good" in the classical Christian sense of that term, then we must recognize that the "no reason" of the hatred goes back to a pride and an enmity, a boredom and an over self-conscious sincerity, which sees in finite, graced human beings a destiny and a being that transcends precisely anything that man can make by or for himself, individually or socially.

Not being surprised by hatred

The political utopias and ecological apocalypses of the recent decades have a common origin in their failure to maintain the centrality of the free person as the axis about which all reality turns. When the person — his natural structural forms and exigencies and his divine destiny — comes to be hated, behind this hatred there lies the mystery of the hatred of the image of God in men. We can call it pride, but it seems more than this. Not merely is it the complete construction of our own self-contained world of whatever model — classless society or Green Earth or what have yc¨ — but it is the positive rejection of whatever caused man to be the kind of real finite creature he is, the one who is sometimes a "son of a bitch", so to speak, the one who too is made in the image of God.

"All men naturally hate one another", Blaise Pascal wrote, deliberately negating a traditional presupposition. Yet, even Paul said that we do hate all men; he did at one time, at least, as he told us in *Titus*. Thus, when we come to reject this hatred, it is through the mystery of divine life which we are given to share, the life that makes us what we are and determines what shall be our good and what our evil, "You must not be surprised, brothers, when the world hates you . . .". And why is it that we must not be surprised? It is because we are free so that even on beholding the good, in our world, in our brothers and in our sisters, in our children, in our works, we need not become good. Machiavelli was right in his perverted shrewdness — hatred is gained as much by good works as by evil ones. The drama of the two Loves building two Cities continues in our own era.

Yet our era has perhaps a certain advantage for we are beginning to witness a profound clarification of alternatives. We are beginning vaguely to recognize that it is the kind of free persons we are created to be that is hated under the ideologies and intellectual constructs of recent centuries. We are not to doubt that out of evil, God can bring good. And it is to some of these works of God, through play and silence and laughter and the love of enemies, that I shall turn in the next section. But we must hold this much firmly, I believe — *we are forbidden to call evil good*. We are forbidden to believe that good develops out of evil such that we must experience the latter to achieve the former. And it is this clarification of good and evil, this "virtue", as it were, that we can find in the "hatred" we so sadly witness. For it does force us to rediscover the fragile concrete person underneath all the movements and philosophies.

Every generation, every life, no matter what its circumstances, is given enough for glory or damnation. We must reject out of hand the oft repeated slogan that some life is not worth living because of its poverty or its oppression or its dullness or its deformity. The rediscovery of the image of God in each man and woman (every person born

95

into the world is an absolute who transcends the world in spite of all the statistics to the contrary), the denial that we *are* evil, even though we are free to do evil, this is the task that Christianity is more and more called upon to perform. No one else can do it, for no one else really believes it. This is why we have so much hatred, when we are given so much grace. For men *can* turn away from the good and call it evil. The place of hatred in Christianity is, then, a fundamental one. For, as John told us, it is often the criterion by which darkness reveals the light. We are to be known, ultimately, as much by what we hate as by what we love.

NOTES

[1] *Corriere della Sera,* 14 Marzo 1977.
[2] Cf. Aquinas, I-II, 29, 1.
[3] Augustine, *The City of God.*
[4] Cf. Aquinas, II-II, 34, 1.
[5] Cf. Aquinas, *Contra Gentiles,* "Quod Deus nihil odit, nec odium alicuius rei ei convenit", I, 96.
[6] London, Collins, 1946, pp. 6-7.
[7] J.V. Schall, *Human Dignity and Human Numbers,* Alba House, New York, 1971.
[8] Cf. Aquinas, II-II, 162, 6 and 7.
[9] Cf. Aquinas, II-II, 34, 2.

Part III

WHAT SAVES US

Chapter VII

ON LONELINESS AND SILENCE

We are fallen men in search of glory in the midst of our Green Earth, with its animals and its mountains, oceans and plains, sometimes under flowing clouds that conceal with light dampness the moon and the stars. We have built lovely things and we have invented theories and ideologies that tell us to tear them down and even to hate our brother. The most dangerous of our kind are often quite sincere, while we can be bored with the most marvellous things because we want nothing but what we invent or control for ourselves.

What can save us? We wonder about this. We suspect that there are ways out. We are even tempted to forget it all. We have hints that we are already redeemed somehow, that there is a transcendence even before the end, even within where we are, who we are. We know everything is not useful, and we suspect this may be the first thing it is wise to know. Where do we begin? We begin mostly, I think, in our loneliness and in our silences, in the quiet discovery that we are already persons who bear an image we were somehow given.

I want to begin with a passage from Balzac's novel *Le Père Goriot*, in which Vautrin says this to Eugene de Rastignac: "I want to clarify one thing for you, the position in which you are. But I will do it with the superiority of a man who, after having examined the things here below, has

G

seen that there are only two positions to take: either a stupid obedience or revolt. I obey nothing. Is that clear?"[1] I wish to suggest, at least, that perhaps such are *not* the only alternatives.

The Cistercian Abbey of Casamari was the second founded by the medieval Norman monks when they came to Italy. Its elegant Gothic architecture, its haunting alabaster windows flooding its interior with an indescribable softness, its dignified simplicity make it one of the world's very beautiful places. There are not so many monks there any more, to be sure, so the Abbey church contains within it a sense of abandonment almost, a feeling that mankind, and with it religious men, are about something else which they consider somehow more vital. Yet once inside its enchanting interior, its quiet beauty seems rather more like a judgment, almost a living defiance of the belief that there is ultimately something more important in the cosmos than that for which it stands.

Just outside the door as you enter the church through its ordered cloister is a plaque with the Latin word "SILENTIUM" inscribed on it. And Casamari is indeed a place where silence is the only proper response. In such a subdued, mystical place you really do miss something if you speak. You miss something even if you are with someone else.

I was at Casamari on the seven hundredth anniversary of the death of Thomas Aquinas, who died in 1274 not too far away at Fossanova, the mother abbey of Casamari. In one of the questions on the Trinity, St Thomas said that we cannot properly use the name "solitary" of God because that would take away the "consortium", the communion of the three persons within the Godhead (I, 31, 2). Silence suggests aloneness. Yet God is not solitary, he is not alone.

The ambiguities of loneliness

Something of this same paradox of the full life of God can also be seen from the traditional problem of the solitary and active religious life. Active life was generally to be preferred because of the things to be done. Likewise there were serious difficulties with a pure contemplative life. Man is normally and naturally a social being, made for friendship and communication. A solitary person was thought to be sufficient to himself; he had to be already perfect. Yet how can a person who is by nature social become perfect alone? Yet the ancient thinkers felt that solitary contemplation was so important that man should devote his whole being to it if he could.

Thus it was concluded, there were only two ways available for such solitary perfection to contemplate God — by divine gift and by virtuous acts. This latter was only possible with the aid of society, both to teach what we do know of God and to reprimand our faults. Thus such a contemplative life was held in great esteem when taken up properly. But it was a very dangerous life unless grace supplied what was lacking. Thus while God is not alone and humans are naturally social, there is still in the medieval and Christian tradition a kind of priority to a solitary life of contemplation because it is a life devoted directly to God.[2]

Yet there is always a frank recognition of the danger of a solitary, contemplative life. Modern sociology and psychology are, of course, full of this danger worked out in the history of modern times. Every one has still heard of *The Lonely Crowd*. Loneliness and solitude are often looked upon as scourges and aberrations. Paul VI wrote: "Man is experiencing a new loneliness; it is not in the face of hostile nature which it has taken him centuries to subdue, but in an anonymous crowd which surrounds him and in which he feels himself a stranger".[3]

Moreover, spiritual literature has long used aloneness to be the image of what is *against* God. Even though Lucifer has a kingdom of sorts, his symbol is that of utter aloneness. Pride, the great sin I spoke of previously, is also conceived in terms of self-sufficiency and aloneness, a world requiring nothing more than one's own constructs. For the Greeks in ancient times, self-sufficiency had been the sign of the city, not of the individual who was incomplete without civic life.

Balzac's Vautrin is, in a way, a good symbol of the man who depends upon and believes only in himself. He is a man who is completely alone even in his friendships, which he valued because all was subordinated to and a product of his desire for absolute independence. Yet the classic religious solitary and Balzac's Vautrin are exactly alike in every sense except that the sole justification of the solitary saint, the man apart from society, is divine grace, that is, complete self-insufficiency. This is why a solitary religious life is such a dangerous pre-eminence since it is so easy, apparently, to dispense with the grace and obey only oneself.

The famous Viennese psychologist, Alfred Adler, once noted that all of the heroes of the Russian novelist Dostoyevsky strove to come to truth through falsehood; they pursued their falsehoods to their very limits. In this pursuit, the realization came that pursuit of power and vice was finally limited by the love of one's neighbour.[4] This ultimately returned the powerful heroes to the limits imposed by human nature so that a life of heroism and love of neighbour could be found in the same person. In this sense, the life of the man who pressed all human vices to their ultimate limits was saved by his realization of a connection with others. This private life was saved by others.

Central spiritual realities

Loneliness, solitude and silence, then, are conceived both as necessary, even central, spiritual realities while, at the same time, they have become symbols of everything inhuman and ungodly. The lonely crowd of the sociologist's description of the modern city, as well as the terrible aloneness of the theological analysis of pride and rebellion, the ultimate rejection of all but the self, have made us aware of the profound danger which comes from cutting oneself off from the society of others.

In one sense, the aberrations of loneliness seem obvious enough. In fact, the modern search for personal communication and love, be it via encounter groups, religious community, modern communication arts, or traditional friendship, has become so pressing that places and opportunities for silence and solitude have become ever rarer in our modern cities and countrysides. Loneliness, furthermore, is seen as something to escape from as quickly as possible, whereas it should have a fundamental place in our personal lives.

"The majority of men live without being thoroughly conscious that they are spiritual beings — and to this is referable all the security, contentment with life . . . which is precisely despair", Kierkegaard wrote in the last century in his *Sickness Unto Death*.[5] This, of course, is one side of Augustine's famous cry, "Our hearts are restless until they rest in thee". Any heart that is thoroughly contented in anything less is, to that extent, shallow and cut off from ultimate vision.

In the theology of traditional Christianity, the reality of loneliness, at first sight, had no place. God is trinity with a vital, full, complete life, whose dimensions of love and knowledge are the incomprehensible model of community and friendship.[6] Thus, God is not alone. The call to participate in this divine life of the Godhead is a call not to be lonely forever, though it is not a call that avoids the loneliness of death.

Indeed, the very meaning of the Christian doctrine of heaven gives the assurance, in spite of all possible appearances, that we shall not be by ourselves eternally because God's gift to us is precisely *his* life.

Man is made, consequently, in God's image. *Genesis* said that it was not good for man to be alone. He is a being for whom friendship is the highest experience. Furthermore, man is a person. Each man contains an inexhaustible creativity rooted in the love with which God created him.

In this sense, persons are themselves unique mysteries in search of who they are through their restlessness, their friendships, their silences and their solitudes. "If a man does not know the value of loneliness", Thomas Merton wrote, "how can he respect another's solitude? It is at once our loneliness and our dignity to have an incommunicable personality that is ours, ours alone, and no one else's and will be so forever".[7]

This, then, is why we are never completely happy even when we are completely happy — which is normally during moments of friendship, love, creativity and service. It is because we are made for a friendship, a happiness that does include the persons we know and love in this life as deeply as we are capable, all of this within a context of being infinite persons whose loves can never be fully satisfied by anything in creation or by all of creation itself. Never to be lonely, therefore, is, ultimately, never to be. For it means that we are not yet aware of what we lack.

Sense of loneliness

In Kyoto, Japan, there is a beautiful and famous rock garden in the Ryoanji Temple. This garden is quite large within a kind of patio enclosure. It consists of some fifteen rocks of various dimensions and shapes jutting up out of meticulously raked sand. About the base of the rocks usually some moss grows. It is conceived to be and is, when you see it, a place of solitude and meditation. When I had a chance to see it all too briefly several years ago, I was immediately struck by the sense of loneliness that it conveyed, yet a loneliness that somehow managed to reveal a sense of astonishment, of discovery and wonder, a feeling of lasting peace.

D.T. Suzuki remarked that a sense of "eternal loneliness" pervades Japanese culture and art and ceremony. His description of the need of this element in our lives deserves long reflection:

When travelling is made too easy and comfortable, its spiritual meaning is lost. This may be called sentimentalism, but a certain sense of loneliness engendered by travelling leads one to reflect upon the meaning of life, for life is after all a travelling from one unknown to another unknown. In the period of sixty, seventy, or eighty years allotted to us we are meant to uncover if we can the veil of the mystery. A smooth running over this period, however short it may be, robs us of this sense of Eternal Loneliness.

. . . You must have seen the picture somewhere in your trip through Japan of a monk in his travelling suit, all alone, looking at Mount Fuji. I forget who the painter was, but the picture suggests many thoughts, especially in the mysterious loneliness of human life, which is, however, not the feeling of forlorneness, nor the depressive sense of solitariness, but a sort of appreciation of the mystery of the absolute.[8]

This, of course, is something that a Christian tradition cannot but profit from. Within the kind of graced life we have been given and promised, there is necessarily the search for the origin of this luminous sensation that nature and persons give to us.

The world is created through the Word, as the Gospel of John tells us. The rocks piercing out of the sand somehow astound us and leave us both at peace and intrigued. They just happened this way, and yet . . . they have an order somehow. The same is true of the human persons we encounter. They all and each are mysteries within a greater mystery. The fact that we cannot create or consume them is a sign, a guarantee that the world is not only ours, that our personhood is already something beyond us. Both Moses on the Mountain and Christ in the Garden of Olives witness to the fact that personhood is first a relation with God, from whom it draws vigour and life. The constant discovery of only the human and the human-made is the bold description of despair, an alienation transcended only by the perception of spirit, the sense of a word calling us through nature and friendship.

We are fools

"The eternal silence of these infinite spaces frightens me", Pascal also wrote in a famous passage. Yet he went on, "we are fools to depend upon the society of our fellowmen. Wretched as we are, powerless as we are, they will not aid us; we shall die alone". This fright of spaces and this powerlessness of society, nevertheless, are signs of insufficiency. In Scripture, Pascal went on, "God is a hidden God, and, since the corruption of nature, he has left men in a darkness from which they can escape only through Jesus Christ, without whom all communion with God is cut off. Nobody knows the Father except the Son and he to whom the Son has wished to reveal him".[9] And John says in his prologue that all things were made in the Word and that the Word was made flesh.

Loneliness, solitude, silence, the hidden God, then, are essential parts of our world. Whatever joy and love we receive, and it is much, is rooted in the paradox that all loves and all knowledges leave us unsatisfied. This can be dangerous and frighten us, to be sure, when it results in our despair and pride, in our boredom and hatred, in our refusal to grant the joy and pleasure of things as they are given to us. Yet a certain solitude and silence is the sign of our dignity. Eternal loneliness is the perceptive admission that nothing we discover in the world suffices, nor is it intended to suffice, though everything is intended to be lovely and good. Deserts and beaches and mountain tops, even infinite spaces, along with quiet churches and haunting rock gardens are places we need to rediscover so that our loneliness is not a sickness unto death nor a despair but rather the result of a gift and a promise to share the life of the hidden God to whom we cannot give the name "solitary".

The biggest human temptation is not to be ambitious

for too much, but to settle for too little. The destructiveness of pride simply consists in assuming the whole world is our classification and creation, even while it obeys its own laws.

One of the fragments left by Meister Eckhard says: "In limpid souls God beholds his own image; he rests in them and they in him. As I have often said, I like best those things in which I see most clearly the likeness of God. *Nothing in all creation is so like God as stillness"*.[10] And the reason stillness is like God is, as a friend once told me who had spent a winter week in St Francis' lonely grotto above Assisi, that "You can hear snowflakes falling *if you listen"*. It is because our affairs are unworthy to be confused with the life we are to live and share. In stillness, in loneliness, in solitude, we learn that our unworthiness is our glory. For it frees us from the only thing we must ultimately be freed from — our belief that the only sound in the universe is the sound we make ourselves in our speeches and in our fabrications, and even in our dances and loves and prayers.

The silence of the infinite spaces frightens me.

I obey nothing — is that clear?

The limits of power intoxication are bound by the love of one's neighbours.

The object really worthy of all serious and blessed effort is God.

"Yahweh came down on the Mountain of Sinai, on the mountain top, and Yahweh called Moses to the top of the mountain . . ." (Ex 19:20).

You must have seen the picture somewhere in your trip through Japan of a monk in his travelling suit, all alone, looking at Mount Fuji . . .

It is not good for man to be alone.

Our hearts are restless . . .

The plaque outside the door at Casamari reads: SILENTIUM.

The word, "solitary", is not to be applied to God.

There is nothing in all creation so like God as stillness.

NOTES

1. *Le Père Goriot,* Paris, Livre de Poche, 1972, p. 124
2. Cf. Aquinas, II-II, 188, 8, and ad 5.
3. *Octogesima Adveniens,* ¶10.
4. *The Practice and Theory of Individual Psychology,* Littlefield, Adams, 1959, pp. 282-83.
5. Doubleday Anchor, 1954, p. 159.
6. Cf. J.V. Schall, *Redeeming the Time,* Sheed and Ward, 1968, Chapter 3.
7. *No Man Is an Island,* Dell, 1957, p. 237.
8. *Zen Buddhism,* Doubleday Anchor, 1956, p. 285.
9. *Pensées,* Dutton, 1957, pp. 202, 206, 242.
10. Harper Torchbooks, R. Blackney, editor, 1957, p. 243.

Chapter VIII

ON THE LOVE OF ENEMIES

So what saves us? The beginning, I suspect, is something outside of ourselves, the realization of a beautiful thing perhaps, something that we did not know existed before, or with the dead end of our hatreds and our pride, or with a sincerity that leaves only our bored selves to be sincere about. Or it may begin in loneliness and silence, in an experience in which we begin to hear in the stillness above the noise. But we have been given a most difficult command in all of this, one we cannot avoid forever. It is not just that we are to hate evil and do good in the concrete persons and world in which we exist. More than that, we are told even to love our enemies, to do good to those who hate us. Imagine! If we are surprised that the world hates us, we are even more astonished to be asked, even commanded, to love our enemies.

In the *Gospel of Luke*, I have often read: "But I say to you who are listening: Love your enemies, do good to those who hate you, bless those who curse you, pray for those who treat you badly" (6: 27-28). How is this even conceivable? How even possible? What does it mean, anyhow?

No doctrine in Christianity is more baffling than that of the forgiveness and love of enemies, not even that of the forgiveness of sins. Not merely is it true that very few people actually seem to have loved their enemies in practice, but even the theory seems quite dubious. Initially, no doubt, the command to love our enemies was intended to shock, to go against what appeared to be a self-evident truth. But what, after all, is the purpose of the love of our enemies?

Instinctively almost, we are inclined to presuppose some very practical purpose, some concrete benefit to ourselves, to society, or even to our enemy. In both Luke and Matthew however, the reasons given for loving our enemy have to do rather with the intrinsic difficulty of the task itself. "If you love those who love you, what right have you to claim any credit?" Christ appears to have recommended this curious love as a kind of test of insurmountable difficulty.

The "love of an enemy" seems to bear none of the reciprocity we normally associate with love. It is a very one-sided affair. No bond between the one who loves and the one who is loved seems to exist. Indeed, the enemy who is loved will not necessarily recognize the love borne to him at all. He may even suspect it to be *hate*. In his capacity as enemy, then, this love will likely be distorted to come across as hypocrisy or naïveté or weakness. But this does not change the situation. For the Christian there is even a certain rejoicing in not being properly loved in return, a sense of suffering with Christ crucified when he received only hatred for his sacrifice.

The spiritual life of the individual

We are, then, to turn the other cheek and to "lend without any hope of return" (Lk 5:34). This violates the elementary norms of justice and even undermines the whole notion of law and public order. Yet, what we seem to be doing, both in Matthew and Luke, is demonstrating that we are sons of God, a conclusion that again makes us wonder what sort of a being the God is who would even suggest such a thing. In any case, the reason is "for he himself is kind to the ungrateful and the wicked". Thus, why we should be kind and bountiful and generous to our enemies is *not* that our considerateness will be a sort of instrumental cause to convert them to a better life. The love of enemy does not seem to be a tool to make the world better. There seems to be no hint that the world is as bad as it is *because* enemies are not sufficiently loved to change them all to the good. God loves the wicked and the ungrateful more than we can, yet they evidently go right on being wicked and ungrateful.

The love of enemy has something to do with our relation to God, our direct relation to God without any mediation of society or neighbour. We have somehow become so accustomed to believing that fulfilling the Christian precepts will make things visibly better in the world that we are almost incapable of accepting the counter suspicion, the possibility that perhaps it will not. Perhaps the worldly response to Christian life both personally and corporately may create a Kingdom *not* of God. Men can, after all, really hate the good in this world, as we have seen. And so the love of our neighbour may in fact demand a rejection of the Kingdom of This World.

Solzhenitsyn wrote in *August 1914:*

 . . . Varosonofiev kept his quarry in his sights. "And if all these *narodinks,* in trying to save nothing less than all the people, refuse to save themselves until that goal is reached? According to their creed, they are forced to. And they are equally forced . . . to regard any one who does not sacrifice himself for the people as worthless — everyone, for instance, who is concerned with art for art's sake or with abstract speculations on the meaning of life, or worst of all, with religion — everyone, in fact, who cultivates and saves his own soul.

 . . . Varosonofiev's resigned yet unwavering stare was capable of kindness . . . Quietly, pausing occasionally, he said: "The word 'develop' has a better and more important application — we should develop our *soul.* There is nothing more precious than the development of a man's own soul; it is more important than the well-being of countless future generations.[1]

The direct relationship of God and human personhood always directly transcends any political or economic order. This is the basic doctrine that much of the social thought of our era is trying to condemn to heresy and oblivion. The love of enemy, I think, maintains the basic sense of transcendence.

Who is our enemy?

In the more practically oriented passages on the love of our enemy, in *Romans* (12:14-21), in *Peter* (1 Pt 3:9) and in Thessalonians (1 Thes 5:15) there is this transcendent notion. "Never repay evil with evil but let everyone see you are only interested in the highest ideals", Paul told the Romans. They were to do all they could to live at peace with everyone and, above all, never to seek vengeance. Paul then cited *Proverbs* (25:21-22), which admonished us to feed the hungry enemy and give him drink. If we should do this, we will "heap read-hot coals on his head". Needless to say, this does not exactly seem cricket. Paul, in fact, left out the conclusion of the original passage in *Proverbs*, which said, "And Yahweh will reward you", almost as if to say that our kindness is a torture to our enemies, a challenge to their ways *and*, on top of it all, a reward to us. Paul then added his own conclusion — "Resist evil and conquer it with good". This passage is almost the essence of the revolutionary new Christian attitude to life. This is more pragmatic. But it is not yet clear if the benefit is for us or for our enemy. Evil is conquered if we do not seek vengeance. The admonition seems primarily directed to our relation to God. We have a personal life with God no matter what our effect on our enemy or on the world.

Who is our enemy? Someone in the New Testament, a lawyer, I believe, did once inquire, "But who then is my neighbour?" His neighbour turned out to be in the Samaritan Parable, the man most in need whom we help. The man beaten by robbers, presumably, did have enemies, namely, the robbers. But he was not the enemy of the Levite or Pharisees or the Samaritan himself. Evidently, no one ever asked, "Who is my enemy?" because this was considered to be obvious. In the New Testament, moreover, the world is never conceived to be populated only with friends and neighbours, of only those who love us. Indeed, the world of only those who love us, of the publicans and sinners, seems rather a dangerous one. The doctrine of the love of enemies is not construed to mean that no enemies exist, that they are an illusion which merely requires some sort of mental therapy to set our vision straight. The New Testament is inexplicable on the grounds that Christ had no enemies, that no one that hated him. If there were no real enemies, the admonition to love them would be sense-less, devoid of objects. Christ's last words, "Father, forgive them for they know not what they do", were not intended to exonerate his executioners but precisely to *forgive* them. If they really did not know in any sense what they did, they would, of course, had no need of forgiveness. Forgive-ness is only operative where there is freedom and violation and knowledge.

Ourselves and our enemies

Rudolf Bultmann remarked that the love of enemies and neighbours is not a detailed recipe. The Old Testament and a Stoic like Seneca admonished us to love our neigh-bour, even to do good to enemies. In the New Testament, "the love of enemies is not the high point of universal love of humanity, but the high point of overcoming of self . . .".[2] The forgiveness of the enemy is a sign of our obedience to God.

For if the thought of forgiveness is taken seriously, this requirement is the most difficult which natural self-love encounters. To remove revenge, to do good to the enemy, even to pray for him — to all this a man can force himself. But to forgive him? This is possible only if one really loves him.[3]

And the number of times we are to forgive is precisely unlimited — seventy times seven (Mt 18:21). This would lead us to suspect that forgiveness and love of enemy do not result in any improvement in the enemy, or at least not necessarily so.

Thus, the love of neighbour and the love of enemy are seen primarily as foundations of the dignity of the human person in his direct relationship to God. The inclusion of the most difficult love of enemy as a sign of our doing what God wills frees us from any social order or any historical time. This is why, in a true sense, all men are equal before God no matter when, where, or under what circumstances they were born and in which they lived. The human person is not dependent upon the world even though he is in it and it affects him. The robbers did thrash and wound the man going from Jerusalem to Jericho. Further, we are to hate what is to be hated. It would be a disorder, a wrong, to love our enemy in so far as he is our enemy — that is, as someone who did something wrong as such.

The love of enemies does not make the good to be evil or the evil to be good. The purpose of the love of our enemy is not some esoteric confusion that clouds our vision about the distinction between good and evil. What is evil is to be hated. There is no other proper response. The love of enemies is not to be confused with the love of evil. The love of enemies is quite different from saying that whatever the enemy does is good to such an extent that our motive in loving is precisely this supposed good under whatever guise. We do not abandon judgment, distinction and value when we love our enemy. We do not pretend to him that his evil really is good.

Hatred in our time has almost ceased to be personal —

which is probably its main horror. It is technological and designed often to solve a social issue. Getting ride of the bourgeoisie is seen as a logical solution to an intellectual impasse. Corporate guilt, that destructive, non-Christian concept when it makes group fault to be personal fault, has never been more in evidence, disguised in its ideological or political formula. Revenge and envy, lurking under many forms, have become the operative principles of many national and party structures. The love of enemies is looked upon as an absurdity. And yet, the kind of unprincipled vengeance wrought in so many cases seems almost visible proof that this love is needed even in political terms.

Is love of enemies a weakness?

Nietzsche, who was in some ways the modern founder of the belief that the love of enemies was against humanity, thought that this Christian virtue of meekness, of turning the other cheek, forgiving our enemies, was ruinous of human value. Nietzsche's condemnation of Christ is illuminating:

> This 'bringer of glad tidings' died as he had lived . . . He does not resist, he does not defend his rights, he takes no step to ward off the worst; on the contrary he *provokes* it. And he begs, he suffers, he loves *with* those, *in* those, who do him evil. *Not* to resist, *not* to be angry, *not* to hold responsible but to resist not even the evil one — to love him.[1]

For Nietzsche this characteristic of Christian practice ends up by approving even evil, which is, of course, the very opposite of its thrust. In this view, then, man must be defined in terms of something beyond man but not in terms in which Christianity has defined him.

The Christian conception of God — God as God of the sick, God as a spider, God as spirit — is one of the

115

most corrupt conceptions of the divine ever attained on earth. It may even represent the low-water mark in the descending development of divine types . . . God — the formula for every slander against 'this world', for every lie about the 'beyond!' God — deification of nothingness, the will to nothingness pronounced holy.[5]

Thus, the Christian God is looked upon as the very antithesis of humanity. And it is precisely this unforgiving public world that has come to be. Yet this is the very world that has almost a physical need of forgiveness, even for its own sake.

The late Hannah Arendt held that forgiveness is, in fact, *the* public virtue of Christianity, not its weakness as Nietzsche held. Love itself, either of friend or foe, is a private thing that transcends the human world. But forgiveness is the one reality that allows peace to settle amidst those peoples who do have a cause for hatred.

> In this respect, forgiveness is the exact opposite of vengeance . . . In contrast to revenge, which is the natural, automatic reaction to transgression and which . . . can be expected and even calculated, the act of forgiving can never be predicted; it is the only reaction that acts in an unexpected way and thus retains . . . something of the original character of action.
>
> Forgiving . . . is the only reaction which does not merely re-act but acts anew and unexpectedly, unconditioned by the act which provoked it and therefore freeing from its consequences both the one who forgives and the one who is forgiven. The freedom contained in Jesus' teachings of forgiveness is the freedom from vengeance . . .[6]

Thus there is a sense in which "justice" is a terrible virtue. And it is no accident that in recent years it has been often preached over charity. Nation after nation seeks to eliminate any cause for "charity" in its midst. Each wants to be absolutely self-sufficient and self-contained in a world where this is possible to no one.

The current passion for justice which we find in ideological and religious circles is, ultimately, I suspect, a formula for disaster in its current forms. For justice, as Plato also realized at the end of *The Republic*, cannot be fully accomplished in this world. There will ever be somehow cause for hatred, greed, turmoil. Furthermore, our desires are precisely unlimited and subjectively defined, so that we will never really receive all we think "due" to us. This is why the social justice theories of recent years, by overlooking this darker side of justice, have deliberately downplayed the role of charity, which was so emphasized in Christian social thought until recently. But there is a sense in which justice tends to bring forth the worst in us. Justice emphasizes exploitation, greed and envy. The world often can come to be seen as a narrow, confined place — not one open and vast, capable of going beyond any existing order in which the content of justice is legally defined.

Thus it is precisely these hate-causing potentialities, almost always presented under the covering of justice, that must be overcome. It is easy to see the injustice of the enemy in terms in which his utter destruction seems the only logical solution to the problem of justice itself. Christianity stands for the belief that justice is inadequate in itself, that the love of enemies and their forgiveness are the only ways to prevent our injustices from proceeding *ad infinitum* in the social order, the reparation of each unjust act becoming in its turn a new cause for hatred and further injustice.

Augustine wrote: "What is the meaning of not returning evil for evil, if not to have an abhorrence for the lust for revenge? And that is to prefer to forgive injuries rather than to seek vengeance, and is simply to forget injuries...". This is not to deny injustices, but precisely to forgive them, to stop a public process that will not stop if we seek to return what was given. In this sense, the Christian

117

is asked to do more than the non-Christian. Men are not equal. Some do more, some are called to do more, some are capable of doing more. The non-Christian who refuses to believe in forgiveness or the Christian who refuses to practise it, each is caught in an unending web of vengeance and righteousness.

The paradox of the love of enemies

In this context, then, the full paradox of the love of enemies comes full circle. The failure to love our enemies continues an action in the world that cannot by itself cease. It goes on from one generation to another, one person to another. Yet victorious enemies think their cause justified precisely by their victory. The essential problem with the love of enemies has ever been: How does it not encourage the very injustices it seeks to stop? It is at this point that justice has ever entered into discussions of charity and forgiveness, even the paradox of loving those we actively punish. Paul was quick to defend his rights, while Jesus himself wanted to know just why he was struck if he did nothing wrong (Jn 18:23). The love of enemies was not designed to promote further hatred and injustice. But it does appear to be true that responding to evil with good can have the dire effect of making the situation worse in worldly terms, at least since the unexpected response of kindness is a further challenge to human freedom which does not necessarily choose the greater good even when confronted with it.

The love of enemies, then, consists in ever treating them as persons, not as causes or groups, exploiters or whatever. But it does not mean we should turn a madman loose on society — the very first problem with justice Plato worried about in *The Republic* and therefore the very beginning of formal political thought. There is, moreover, no *reason* to love our enemy. Our enemy is precisely unloveable *as* enemy. It would be false to pretend otherwise. The love of enemy must include a belief in the human freedom to cease doing what is wrong. This is why the love of enemy is almost the ultimate challenge we can give to men.

The love and forgiveness of enemies, we know, is the direct will of God. It partakes in a providence, something that transcends our personal lives but which operates through and because of them. And loving our enemy does not mean that he will immediately change his way because of our virtue. If this were so, we would gladly love our enemies on purely pragmatic grounds. The love of enemies is, in this sense, a "weakness", as it were, because it does not do what it ought, what is just. To do more than justice is, in a very vivid sense, "unjust". Yet this alone can stop the eternal cycle of vengeance and retaliation. No other solution has so far been discovered. Justice by itself is ever a dead-end street. "Make sure people do not try to take revenge", Paul wrote to the Thessalonians. "You must all think of what is best for each other and the community" (1 Thes 5:14). This is also found in *Leviticus*: "You must not exact vengeance, nor must you bear a grudge against the children of your people. You must love your neighbour as yourself" (19:18).

The New Testament, then, reaffirms and takes up what is found in the Old Law. Christ added to this that we should love one another as he loved his Father and his friends — even unto death. He did not call his enemies "his friends" except in the case of Judas when he said to him, sadly, "My friend, what are you here for?" (Mt 26:50). The love of enemies is not designed to obliterate the distinction of justice and injustice, of good and evil. Nor is it designed directly to "convert" our enemy, even though it may "heap red-hot coals on his head" for not recognizing the profundity of the call of God. The love of enemies will not necessarily change the world, just as it did not seem to have changed Judas.

Yet even on empirical grounds, it seems to be the one thing that the world must possess if it is to be at peace with itself. We do not love our enemies for any reward our enemies or even our friends give but for the reward that God gives. This is important because it is the one truth that enables us to transcend any nationalism, ideology, religion, philosophy, or personal injustice that locks us into ourselves. We are saved ultimately by God, not by the world from which we have no assurance. The love of enemies becomes more and more the only thing that can save us — even in this world. That is why, perhaps, it is not of this world.

NOTES

[1] New York, Bantam, 1974, pp. 469, 473. Cf. also pp. 630-31.
[2] *Jesus and the Word*, New York, Scribner's, 1958, p. 112.
[3] *Ibid.*, p. 116.
[4] The Antichrist, ¶35, *The Portable Nietzsche*, Kaufmann, editor, New York, Viking, 1954, pp. 608-9.
[5] *Ibid.*, ¶18, pp. 585-86.
[6] *The Human Condition*, Doubleday Anchor, 1959, p. 216.

Chapter IX

ON SADNESS AND LAUGHTER

Loneliness and silence, the love of enemies, such are the ironicals ways we are given to find our way out of ourselves, our envies and our hatreds and our pride. Sadness at the good, just for its being good, boredom with what is, in fact, fascinating, reveals much of what we are to ourselves. And this possibility that we should hate the good or be bored with it, I have worried, is a kind of a sign of the reality of our freedom, its real possibility for rejecting the delight of the good. This is not the least reason why our histories are filled with a vast drama that includes failure and tragedy, for there is much at stake.

Yet there is perhaps another kind of sadness, not one so much angered or depressed about the good, but one which realizes the good that is all about us, one that sees it pass away so quickly, one that is touched by our human lot, one based on our finiteness and fallenness. Back in the Spring of 1971, the Ecole Normale Superieure in Paris was closed for a spell by another of those government-student-faculty-administration crises which have so bedevilled our recent years. Among the graffiti on the wall were found, as Oliver Todd told us at the time, "These warmed over phrases from May, 1968":

Le mot est haissable!
La violence est la commencement du debut de la fin!
Nous abolirons la tristesse! [1]

Each of these slogans (were they really so random, I wondered) struck me in their contrast. "The word is hateful — In the beginning was the Word". "Violence inaugurates the beginning of the beginning of the end — The Alpha and the Omega". "We shall abolish sadness . . .".

This latter proclamation, in this context, I could not quite eradicate from my memory. Somehow it seemed to me to be the most hopeless thing I have ever seen, however much like joy it might have sounded. This was not the sadness about the good being good, but the actual claim to abolish sadness. I began to wonder if sadness was not something more positive than I had suspected. I recalled the beatitude — "Blessed are those who mourn, for they shall be comforted" (Mt 5:4). But even more I remembered laughter and comedy. In one way or another, through the maze of our sanity, this bold challenge of a new era on a French wall struck at the very depths of our humanity. For it attacked, unknowingly perhaps, the roots of our laughter. Instinctively almost, I knew this was the really crucial issue. For I can accept humanity and its sadness because I believe in laughter.

Among the other eternal negligences on my part, I had never managed to read P.G. Wodehouse. Then one spring I bought a second-hand copy of *Right-Ho Jeeves* — of such are my finances and chances. I bought it mainly as a pledge against my considerable capital of ignorance for I am, in fact, a hopeful man. But as with so many books we buy, I was not really sure that the day would ever come to redeem my pledge. And this is all right, of course, for the greatest gifts we have been given are the many things we shall never know. It seems, however, that providence, or whatever it is that governs our accidents, is on my side. For the night before I chanced to read the French slogans, I began to read Wodehouse.

Enough sadness in life

The employer of Jeeves, one Bertram Wooster, had an old school friend, it seems, with the highly unlikely name of Augustus Fink-Nottle. This Fink-Nottle, who was called "Gussie" for short, was evidently a very bashful, retiring sort of a chap who spent most of his time at his country estate engaged in observing newts. One afternoon, however, on a walk he had made the acquaintance of a young friend of "Bertie's" (for such she called Bertram) Aunt Dahlia and had fallen in love with the young lady. Totally inexperienced in such affairs of the heart and the world, the shy newt-watcher sought some advice from Jeeves.

Rising to the occasion, this sage butler of Wooster had advised Gussie to attend the local costume ball where the said young lady would be present. The crux of Jeeves' advice, however, was that to draw the young miss's attention, he should not appear at the ball in some ordinary outfit like that of Pierrot the Clown, but rather in the red tights and black mask of Mephistopheles himself. Fink-Nottle explained Jeeves' reasoning clearly to Wooster:

"Yes, Jeeves is a great believer in the moral effect of clothes. He thinks I might be emboldened in a striking costume, like this. He said a Pirate Chief would be just as good. In fact, a Pirate Chief was his first suggestion, but I objected to the boots".

I saw his point. There is enough sadness in life without having fellows like Gussie Fink-Nottle going about in sea boots.[2]

"We will abolish sadness — There is enough sadness in life . . .". How utterly different are these two attitudes towards our condition! P.G. Wodehouse, it seems, is by far the greater revolutionary, for he saw clearly what perhaps only humorists see clearly, that sadness is, ultimately, not something to be "abolished" from our human midst, but rather it is something at the very centre of our condition without which our joy and our laughter somehow would not really be ours, would not even be possible.

Walter Kerr, likewise, has noted this curious connection between sadness and laughter, not the sadness over the good, but the sadness that this good world passes away. Commenting on a biography of Bert Lahr, Kerr wrote:

> There are agreeable, even light-hearted glimpses of Beatrice Lillie at work, of Fred Allen being friendly, of Abe Burrows being generous, of vaudevillians summering at Lake Hopatcong, of a fund-raising wartime caravan of stars gathering nightly in Laurel and Hardy's dressing room. But the dominant tone is otherwise: Beatrice Lillie is crying, Oliver Hardy is trying hard not to. By the time you are through with the book you may have the feeling that you might just cry yourself.
>
> For we are brought very close to a man who was himself close to the dark heart of comedy . . .[3]

This is a very astonishing, provocative phrase — the dark heart of comedy — almost as if there were something frightening, occult even, connected with humour. In fact, Walter Kerr even said that when we look at the true comic, we are indeed "looking at terror".

How utterly paradoxical this all seems that those who wish to abolish sadness must also in their course abolish laughter, while those who see the terror in the dark heart of comedy are the ones who give us joy and cheer. And yet this is the case, for our human joys are predicated precisely on the sufficiency of sadness in life that does not need fellows like Gussie Fink-Nottle going about in sea boots. Furthermore, though there may indeed be joys higher than our human ones (which are themselves, if we know them, higher even than our fondest dreams) still for men, these higher joys are not to be achieved apart from that sadness which gives rise to our laughter. In other terms, we shall only abolish sadness by abolishing what we are.

Loving bad jokes

On Palm Sunday some years ago now, a friend wrote a letter which I received a month later — such is the cosmic time it took to travel two kilometres through the annual, all-too-human Italian postal strike. The letter ended: "Did you know that (former Mayor John) Lindsay has referred to New York's 'fiscal crunch' so many times that several reporters are considering asking him for the recipe? *I love bad jokes . . .*". Sometimes I feel, this is the ultimate freedom — that of loving bad jokes since, in a way, this is what we all are, rather bad jokes in search of being loved. This is the real terror that the comic sees, around which he dances for us all to laugh. What our faith is really about is very simple — that there is in truth someone to laugh with us, that the bad jokes we really are, really are loved. This is why, in a sense, comedy is more profound than tragedy.

The beginning of the beginning of the end

Yet what I am saying concerns not only sadness and humour, but also "The beginning of the beginning of the end" — words with obvious apocalytpic overtones. For there is a kind of visionary radicalism fervently preached today in many quarters, a radicalism unwilling to tolerate the imperfect world of men, a revolutionary spirit which passes quickly from peace to violence and violence to peace, all in the name of the new and more perfect end said to be beginning. "The world is hateful". This is not to be totally unexpected, of course. The Manicheans in Augustine's time hated the world. Violence in Greek thought meant precisely the area prior to speech, prior to politics. And there is an ancient saying which goes, "A happy country has no history".

In other words, then, rapid passage from violence to peace and back again, all of an afternoon, is absolutely logical when we have bypassed our frailties and our absurdities, when we have forgotten that men are themselves somehow bad jokes, loved and laughed at from generation to generation. The enemy of laughter has always been a kind of utopia — be it the utopia of the mystic radicals or of the secret police. I believe in God mainly because his revelation has rejected both. In my view, the bad joke is the greater vision.

The noted Italian journalist, Guido Piovene, once wrote a series of articles on contemporary Denmark. At the end of his trip, he sighed:

> I returned to Copenhagen to pass my last night there before going down to Germany. I am about to leave a sympathetic country — one poised between rationalism and fairy tales, a country I should like to know better.
>
> Wishing to go to bed early, I had dinner in an almost deserted restaurant. There was soft music. Outside the windows, a stop-light passed from red to green, from green to red. Before me was a panorama of empty tables, all with immaculately white table cloths, all with a vase of tulips, a lamp with a red shade, a long, lighted candle. The mournful sound of sirens came from the sea. I felt I had become a little mediocre — like the tubercular traveller of the "Belle Epoque" in a melancholy mood which does not succeed in achieving sadness.[4]

The abolition of sadness meant ironically not happiness and joy, but rather melancholy and dullness — such, as I have hinted, is the true destiny of our contemporary revolutions whose intellectual content is such that it will reduce us all to a pitiable sameness, stop-lights vacillating from red to green, green to red forever and ever.

Tragic and laughable figures

Piovene's analysis of Denmark, of course, is nothing less than Thomas Mann. The melancholy tubercular of the "Belle Epoque" is *The Magic Mountain*. The sad Dane is Tonio Kröger. But there is in Thomas Mann, I believe, something about Denmark that Piovene missed. A Danish friend once told me in Hümlebak that there is also a certain gaiety to the Danes . . . Tonio Kröger concludes:

As I write, the sea whispers to me and I close my eyes. I am looking into a world unborn and formless, that needs to be ordered and shaped; I see into a whirl of shadows of human figures who beckon me to weave spells to redeem them: Tragic and laughable figures, and some that are both together — and to these I am drawn. But my deepest and most secret love belongs to the blond and blue-eyed, the fair and living, the happy, lovely and commonplace.[5]

I see, in other words, that the real issue of our time is whether the commonplace and the ordinary, the sadness and the laughter of the human lives we are given (a sadness and laughter based on our anxieties and our talents, on our vanity and our limitations, on our birth and on our death) are to prevail.

The beginning of the beginning of the end — We shall abolish sadness . . . The notion of "the end of history" has become, as Eric Weil remarked, a key idea in recent revolutionary thought. The end of history has come to mean more particularly that man now actually has it in his power to abolish and eradicate those evils of violence, injustice, and suffering that occur in the natural and social orders. In the future, man will be subject only to those types of evils that he himself chooses — that is, there will still be tragedy, if not comedy.

The end of history . . . is the end of the oppression which prevents men from holding themselves open for what is, in natural right, always at their disposition. It does not signify that there will no longer be events or that men will no longer die or that all love will necessarily be happy, all children gifted, all men good and beautiful. Further, it does not mean that after the end of history there can no longer be tragedies and suffering for the individual. On the contrary, the individual is defined by the fact that he is always exposed to conflicts, to deceptions . . . But the evils of a free and reasonable man in a free and reasonable world will be his own evils . . ."[6]

Thus there will be no more tragedy due to exploitation, social events, poverty, wars, insufficient education, false careers but only that of the person who deliberately chooses evil and hence tragedy for himself. We shall then abolish sadness only to be able to return to choose it freely and reasonably at the end of history. We shall choose it no longer under the appearance of a good which might somehow humanly excuse us but only for its naked self.

The touch of madness

But are tragedies ever purely individual and private? Are bad jokes to be kept from the masses? The attempt to achieve a free and reasonable humanity liberated from all technical, historical and political oppressions presumes that what goes on in our own private hearts will have no public effect. Further, it also presupposes that someone somewhere will be separate and apart enough in the public order to rule without the taint of sin and finiteness. This is precisely what our current revolutionaries — Marxists, post-Marxists, anti-Marxists, and what have you — claim to be achieving. But ultimately the only way to prevent our private tragedies and comedies from affecting the world is to deny us our tragedies and comedies. This is why the passage through violence to utopia is so often accompanied in practice by the police state.

Yet not even the new public order will rest quietly. We are not merely at "the end of history" but, as the Italian sociologist Luciano Gallino once told a Pugwash Conference at Frascati, we are at "the end of the myth of science considered as a human power intrinsically beneficial, directed toward dominating nature and society".[7] Thus at the precise moment when the public and scientific world claims to save us from moral and physical evil and tragedy, that very same world is seen to turn against man.

And the private world of the revolution which has rejected any established public order because so far it did not abolish sadness and war and poverty and evil is, as Marcia Cavell once argued, a world of both innocence and madness.

The students I have spoken with generally find the idea of guilt unacceptable in every way. They deny the possibility that they may feel it without being aware that they do; they are convinced that the guilt they do feel is nothing but the projection into their consciousness of a false moral system; and they think that in a healthy society we would be guilt-free.[8]

If there is no present guilt, of course, there is no distinction between sanity and insanity, between "public" and "private" realities. With no public world, there is only an aloneness since nothing else is real. And this aloneness which hears nothing, not even itself, begins to erode the very reality of the individual.

The revolutionary's conviction that only societies, not individuals, are culpable blends with the claim of many religions that in a certain sense the individual is not real and that reality is one. The moral and religious insight that man is not God and that human things are always less than perfect is turned on its head: no one is to blame. What begins as a plea for the individual ends as a voiding of that concept altogether, for there are no agents — the plea continues — only victims.[9]

Thus when the infamous Charles Manson, the mass killer, pleaded innocent of what the rest of the world could only call madness, Professor Cavell concluded he did so on the solid grounds of much contemporary religion and revolutionary thought.[10] Again we end up with theories that evaporate the person in the name of the species or collective group, only to end up with nothing ever being the responsibility of a particular human will. And this is the opposite of the Christian instinct.

Violence is the beginning of the end. We shall abolish sadness. Madness comes to be called sanity in a world where the Word is hateful.

Seldom cussing for purely personal reasons

One of W.C. Field's heroes was a Germantown undertaker by the name of Chester Snavley, a wonderful name Fields later used in several of his short films. What impressed Fields was the undertaker's unctuous, absurd, officious funeral for a certain Ernest O. Potts, a performance Fields had seen as a boy. By the time the funeral had reached the cemetery, the hired mourners, the slightly tipsy Wiggins family in carriage number seven, the farmer on the buckboard loaded with limestone blocks who accidentally got caught in the cortège had all made an indelible impression on Fields — so much so that his will later insisted that he be quietly cremated with absolutely no ceremony.

The sermon at the grave was classic, indeed symbolic.

It was a difficult sermon. The family agreed afterwards that the minister had done the best he could with the materials at hand. The truth was that, despite his hearty farewell, Potts had been something of a rip.

Reverend Sumpter pounded away at his good points but at best they had been pretty thin, and in the aggregate, the message took on more or less the tone of an apology. Sumpter said that, although Potts had *not* been active in the church, and in fact was never seen there except on Founder's Day, when he turned up for the free dinner, he had never actually talked *against* it; that, as a good many people knew who abetted him now and then, present company not necessarily excepted, but naming no names, Potts *was* a good deal of a boozer, but he was not a troublesome boozer, and no report had ever come to him (Reverend Sumpter) about the departed having knocked his wife or children around to excess; and that, while he was extraordinarily free with his language, to a point where no sensitive person would care to get within a half a mile of him, he had seldom cussed anybody out for purely personal reasons, but had stuck fairly close to things like politics and sports right down the line.[11]

So it is, perhaps, that this is really our final claim to fame, that our best has been indeed pretty thin, that the best thing that can be said for us at last is delightfully funny, along with the sadness. With Ernest O. Potts, we may never have been excessively active in church but we were never against it. We never cussed anyone out for purely personal reasons. We may really have been rips and boozers, but not especially troublesome ones.

This is what most of us are. At the dark heart of comedy and of reality, we dimly perceive that we are like W.C. Fields' friend Chester Snavley, like Ernest O. Potts and the Wiggins family in carriage number seven, like Bert Lahr and Beatrice Lillie and Oliver Hardy, cosmic bad jokes all, in search of someone to love us, secure in the knowledge that the end of history and sadness will not achieve a greater, more improbable being than what we find about us. By the time we too are ready to find our place in the Germantown Cemetery, with the Reverend Sumpter charitably reciting our faults, we too may feel comforted that those who have followed the procession may indeed feel like crying because there has been laughter all the way.

Blessed are those who mourn, for they shall be comforted. Someday, on a French wall, I hope to write, preferably in red and green like the stop-lights:

Nous acceptons la tristesse! We do accept sadness.

With my friends, I shall continue to love bad jokes. There is indeed enough sadness in life without Gussie Fink-Nottle going about in sea boots.

131

I

NOTES

[1] *Le nouvel Observateur*, 13 Avrvil 1971, p. 38.
[2] Penguin, p. 21.
[3] "An Essay Review of *Notes on a Cowardly Lion*, by John Lahr", *The Saturday Review*, 15 September 1969, p. 33.
[4] *La Stampa*, 18 Aprile 1971.
[5] "Tonio Kröger", *Thomas Mann's Stories and Episodes*, London, Dent, 1940, p. 68.
[6] "La fin de l'histoire", *Revue de Metaphysique et de Morale*, Octobre-Decembre,, 1970, p. 383.
[7] *Corriere della Sera*, 5 Maggio 1971.
[8] "Visions of a New Religion", *The Saturday Review*, 19 December 1971, p. 44.
[9] *Ibid.*, p. 43.
[10] *Ibid.*, p. 44.
[11] R.L. Taylor, *W.C. Fields: His Follies and His Fortunes*, Signet, 1967, p. 118.

Chapter X

ON PLAYING

Thus we are saved too by even our laughter, perhaps especially by it. And by our sadness, when we discover that we too are always dying midst the beauty and our friends; by our enemies even we are saved when we love them. Nor should we be surprised, that, like Ernest O. Potts, each of us probably is also "a bit of a rip", as the Reverend Sumpter said. We have all worn sea boots to make a sadder world laugh. And we have known we were bad jokes who can sing and dance — and yes, play. What saves us in the beginning is our being struck by a beauty we did not know, by finally realizing that there are indeed things beyond use. And our playing is very near to contemplation, as the ancients told us.[1] When we play, we play for its own sake, for the play itself. So we must wonder about this connection between play and contemplation.

In the late 1870's, Samuel L Clemens, as he tells us in his thoroughly wonderful *Life on the Mississippi*, visited St Paul, Minnesota, as a final stop on his nostalgic return to the river that begot him. He noted the flourishing city, its natural beauty, the "unusually fine railroad station", the "wide views of the river and lowlands offered from its streets".

Yet for Mark Twain, the soberness and industriousness of this new section of the most gigantic river valley in the world contained a paradox, indeed a wonderful joke which was almost metaphysical and seemed to stand behind all the grim and noble efforts of man. In truth, Mark Twain was almost Hegelian, but with a more affectionate smile, in his view of the causes at work in history:

> How solemn and beautiful is the thought that the earliest pioneer of civilization, the van-leader of civilization is never the steamboat, never the railroad, never the newspaper, never the Sabbath school, never the missionary — but always whisky! Such is the case. Look history over; you will see. The missionary comes after the whisky . . .[2]

Then, as if to prevent anyone from accusing him of disrespect, Mark Twain slyly distinguished apostolic purpose from mere time sequence — "I mean he arrives after the whisky has arrived".

"The missionary arrives after the whisky" — this deliberate ambiguity about the word "after", this delightful jest at human pretentiousness, enables us to laugh at ourselves and our kind. The noblest of human efforts, the building of cities, have mundane, even comical origins. Such is the *glory* of us men, to return to the theme I began with.

This then is my first proposition: *It is precisely this ability to see humour in serious human effort that saves us.* My second proposition immediately follows: *This capacity only exists in men because it is previously in God.*

The Jester and the Priest

Though I believe he has his cast of characters somewhat confused, I think the Polish philosopher Laszek Kolakowski has sensed some of this in his noted essay, "The Priest and the Jester". For Kolakowski, it is the priest who stands for the seriousness of order, while it is the jester who sees the improbability and foibles of any historical setting.

The priest is the guardian of the absolute who upholds the cult of the final and obvious contained in tradition. The jester is he who, although an habitué of the good society, does not belong to it and makes it the object of his inquisitive impertinence; he who questions what appears to be self-evident . . .

The philosophy of the jester is a philosophy which in every epoch denounces as doubtful what appears as unshakable; it points out the contradictions in what seems evident and incontestable; it ridicules common sense and reads sense into the absurd. . . .[3]

This, I say, somewhat confuses the cast of characters, at least for St Paul — the man, not the city. For the City of St Paul, as Mark Twain jested, began in June 1837, when "Pierre Parrant, a Canadian, built the first cabin, uncorked his first jug and began to sell whisky to the Indians".[4] And it was the man (Paul's master) who said, "Render unto Cæsar the things that are Cæsar's and to God the things that are God's", who really upset the order of tradition.

For Paul, however, "the foolishness of God is wiser than men . . . (and) God chose what is foolish in the world to shame the wise . . ." (1 Cor 1:25, 27). What Paul told Timothy was that the Christian life would appear as foolish while the world would embrace every form of vice and error as if it were wisdom (2 Tim 3 and 4). When Paul spoke at Athens to the citizens and foreigners gathered there who "spent their time in telling or hearing something new", as *Acts* (17:21) tells us, on hearing something so startling new as the resurrection, they merely "mocked" him (17:32). That is, they reacted to Paul as to a jester.

For Paul, then, the real paradox is not "priest *and* jester", but rather "priest as jester", for it is the priesthood of all believers who are to see the foolishness of this world — and laugh. The wisdom of God, therefore, becomes the foolishness of men. The delight of the Christian is precisely caused by the gravity and seriousness of the worldly enterprise which is seen to be foolishness, a thing that causes us laughter in the living of it out.

The convinced Christian believes that his views of reality at once make more sense (that is, are more intellectually satisfying and correct) and result in more joy (that is, are more fundamentally responsible to what achieves his real hope) than any other understanding of reality. For the Christian, all other theological, æsthetic, philosophical and political systems are to be judged by these two criteria: Do they make men more happy? And, by their fruits and faults you shall know them.

On being given a stone when promised a diamond

In this approach, then, Christians tend to be the most ruthlessly "pragmatic" creatures in a way, because they cannot and will not be satisfied with a new wine in a new bottle that is in no wise superior either to the old wine or even to the old bottle. For Christians, the ultimate heresy is the ultimate delusion, to be given a stone when promised a diamond. They know that any theory which pretends that the two are exactly the same thing is lacking in something. For Christians, this something is quite literally everything.

There is an attitude today, of course, that it is merely nostalgic to talk about any such convinced creatures as "convinced" Christians. We presume that the "nobility of doubt" has somehow seized us all. Our contemporaries are often more inclined to believe not that "the missionary came after the whisky" but that the whisky caused the missionary to come in the first place. We all have our difficulties, to be sure. Yet it is the free Christian who pays human reality this supreme compliment: "Live your belief out as best you can", he says, "and let me see what happens to you when you live what you say you believe. Then allow me to judge if I really want to live as you do".

In other words, Christianity has never believed that "sincerity" alone, as I have suggested, really saved a man from disaster. Yet, lest we should forget, Christianity never believed that truth alone would save a man from disaster either. The Cross was a disaster in spite of its truth. The question is, how was this disaster both true and salvific? Even more mysteriously, how was it joyful? For this is what Christian tradition sang about the Cross in hymns. It is precisely the *felix culpa*. For the intellectuals of this world whose imaginations did not allow a broader vision, this doctrine was foolishness. St Paul was quite right. The missionaries could be explained only in terms of the whisky, in terms of foolishness.

For this reason, perhaps, it may not be a sheer accident that the assembled Parthians and Medes and Elamites, the residents of Mesopotamia, Judea and Cappadocia, Pontus and Asia and the rest gathered at Jerusalem said of the Eleven motley fishermen simply, "They are filled with new wine" (Acts 2:13). For we should recall old wine merely makes us mellow, while whisky was not invented for another fifteen hundred years — reason enough, as Belloc said, not to drink it. And so this is my third proposition: *The foolishness of God makes even the wisdom of men a joy because it enables us to see the exaggeration and the distortions of man's own life and thought.* The foolishness of God is that the Cross is somehow a joy. For Thomas à Kempis, the "Royal Road of the Holy Cross" was suffused with *glory*. For it is the wisdom of men that crucifies and the foolishness of God that saves — that saves men precisely from their own wisdom.

So the priest *is* the jester, and the whisky does make the missionary. Yet, how does this make sense, let alone joy? I sometimes think Christian theology has never sufficiently understood its own dogmas, because Christian theologians never sang and danced enough. Nor did they run in the race, as St Paul suggested, to see how it was that only one won the prize.

Yet if we approach Christianity from our singing and our dancing, from our gaming and our twirling, we can, I think, begin to see it in an entirely new light, in a way in which all mystery is heightened precisely because revealed, all its work made effortless, all its pain transformed by expectation. But this is only possible if we recognize that our dreams have been too small and our joys too lame. Indeed, and this is my fourth proposition: *What mainly prevents us from being more complete humans is the smallness of our vision.*

Nothing need exist

The game that life gives us is thus a greater game than the one we invent for ourselves. And yet the main, in fact the only way we know this is that the games we invent for ourselves, our football, our races, our circuses and our slides, never cease to fascinate us. The spectator at the match, the fan who cheers and bets and yells, who wants his team to win yet knows there is to be a final gun, he it is who assures us that what we are for is really beyond what we can produce or make for ourselves. He it is who knows that somehow when we cheer, we want to cheer forever. It is the whistle and the kick-off that begin the game, the final gun that ends it. The beginning and the end, the Alpha and the Omega.

But what is there to cheer forever? We take the world too seriously, too grimly. If we do not believe in God, we must believe in the supreme importance of the world. And the world cannot bear such seriousness. It makes such a small faith. The existence of God frees us from the solemnity of the world. I believe, of course, that the universe is important and so is our enterprise in it. I profess to be a contemporary man. Indeed, I accept and glory in the priority given in *Genesis* and *Colossians*, that man is the reason for the earth and the moon and the stars. I do not indeed know just how widely to extend "man" throughout the universe. There are probably other rational creatures about somewhere. If not, I assume that men will eventually take possession of all the cosmos itself.

Yet, and this is my fifth point: *Nothing in the world, nor the world itself needs to exist.* All this is quite unnecessary. And therefore, all is free. It is, like all our sports, a game that need not have been played at all.

At first sight, of course, this may not seem like anything to cheer about. But it is. Indeed, it is what makes cheering itself possible. For it means that what stands outside of creation is greater than creation. Or to put it another way, the reality and completeness and fullness of the internal life of God is in no wise deficient. Man and creation are not psychological compensations for what God lacks. God does not lack otherness nor friendship. He is revealed as Father, Son and Spirit. Because God is complete, man is free. Because man is free, he stands to God ultimately as a beholder, who can merely utter, as Isaiah tells us, "Holy, Holy, Holy" (6:3).

Often, it seems, God would be greater if man's task in the universe were necessary, necessary to God. But this is not so. Our task is necessary to one another, as to the physical universe itself. We have, furthermore, a real game to play according to rules we did not make — which is, incidentally, usually the case with any game that men play. How we play this ultimate game determines how we shall see God. For you cannot gain the prize if you do not enter the race. The one thing we are not allowed is the chance to reject playing the game. That is the ultimate nothingness which even God does not give us.

Ultimately beholders

But we are ultimately beholders — even of one another. What we have is what we are given. It is not our need for cheering that makes cheering fun and spontaneous. Rather it is that there is first something to cheer about and that we have been invited, as it were, to watch the beginning and the end. It is because we can behold that we can laugh and shout. Plato was not wrong, in one of the most marvellous passages ever written: "And therefore, as we say, everyone of us should live the life of peace as long and as well as he can. And what is the right way of living? Are we to live in sports always? If so, in what kind of sports? We ought to live sacrificing and singing and dancing, and then a man will be able to propitiate the Gods . . ." (*Laws*, ¶803).

To see creation and ourselves as the fantasy and playthings of God as Plato did, then, is relatively easy (*Laws*, ¶644). Nothing "had" to exist. Other worlds are "possible". This is the one that *is* — in which we spend our lives sacrificing and singing and dancing. There is an unutterable delight in standing outside nothingness, no matter how we stand. Dylan Thomas has caught some of this wonder:

> And then to awake, and the farm,
> like a wanderer white
> With the dew, come back, the cock on his shoulder:
> it was all
> Shining, it was Adam and the maiden,
> The sky gathered again
> And the sun grew round that very day.
> So it must have been after the birth
> of the simple light
> In the first, spinning place, the spellbound
> horses walking warm
> Out of the whinnying green stable
> On to the fields of praise.[5]

Proverbs (8:25ff) tells of Wisdom playing before the Lord. And John tells us in his prologue that the Word became flesh, almost as if this were one choice out of many, almost as if, indeed, to accept a challenge.

Running from God is the longest race of all

But how can our evil and our transiency ever be cheered? We have seen Bert Lahr and Oliver Hardy almost crying.

Is not the Dance of Death the only dance we have? If our creation be a game, the rules are rigged. Our lot is surely tragic.

Hugo Rahner, in his memorable book, *Man at Play*, says not only must we see that creation is the play of God but, more importantly, so is redemption. This is a striking thought — though we already know from Sophocles and Aeschylus and Shakespeare that the tragic somehow restores.

Redemption is also the play of God! How so? we wonder. Roger Caillois has tried with considerable success to give us a nomenclature of games.[6] We have, he suggested, four kinds of games — the *agon*, or contest games; the *alea*, or betting games; *mimicry*, or imitation games; and *ilnix*, or vertigo games. Some games, he said, can combine various types. Most card games, poker or bridge, for example, combine chance and skill. We are dealt "a hand" by fate. We then play as best we can.

Man has dealt God a difficult hand. We might object that it is the other way around. But it is not so. What is the truth is that God received a very bad deal. What is the mystery is that he consented to play with the deal he received. Christianity says, and this is my sixth proposition, that *God is winning in spite of the hand he has received.* God will not change the rules of the game. Freedom is the rule and the context of the game.

In other words, the kind of universe we have, the kind wherein men really choose for valuable stakes, and where they often choose badly, is still a place in which they can discover God and cheer. It sounds paradoxical to say that God is beating us at our own game. But the fact is that this is quite theologically accurate. And still, and this is my seventh proposition, *even God need not win everything; there is a real contest about life.*

What is even more surprising, however, is that there are times when we can even enjoy being beaten. We sometimes forget that the athlete knows it is no disgrace to lose when he has played well. Indeed it is a glory. We want the better man to win, even when we lose. We also forget, and this is even more incomprehensible, that the cheat and the spoil-sport, those who refuse to abide by the rules or who even refuse to enter the game, are still being challenged and contested in the checkerboard of life. From God's view, they can never make a move that does not leave them open still to his rules and hence even in losing they can still win.

This is why the images of running or of the "Hound of Heaven" or of the fishermen are not such bad ones. Edmund Fuller quoted Theodore Roethke's poem, ". . . Running from God's the longest race of all".[7] "I fled him down the nights and down the days . . .". Somehow the race or the hunt or the pond describe quite vividly God's game with men. "Behold, I shall make you fishers of men" (Mt 4:19). Curious thing to tell the apostles. Sooner or later, the wiliest old catfish is tossed a morsel he simply cannot resist. Sometimes it is the boy with the night crawler and the bent pin, sometimes it is the professional with the latest artificial lure. Christian theology simply suggests that God is always about looking for this precious bait that will open up even the toughest life. And this is my eighth proposition: *God will not drain the pond to catch the fish, it must always make the first strike.*

E.L. Mascall remarked that the problem of evil and its redemption is rather like the rower on the Cambridge team whose sufferings and strain do not matter because they are forgotten in his "getting to Mortlake Brewery before the Oxford boat".[8] It is easy for us to see, he told us, how such sufferings can be forgotten but how about the great human tragedies, Belsen and Dachau? How can even God forgive them? How can we? The answer lies in the direction of seeing that God's reasons, his field of play, is so much larger than ours; that we exclude possibility for lack of imagination and vision.

We do not remember the strain when the victory is won or even when we lose. It may be that the game we play is a greater one than we suspect. And this is my ninth proposition: *When we substitute our rules in the game of*

life, we always make a less interesting game in the world.
The challenge God gives across the ages is simply this: You
really will enjoy my game more, for its stakes are infinitely
higher and the possibility of winning infinitely greater than
any game you might devise for yourself.

In the *Book of Revelation,* God is the Alpha and the
Omega, the first and the last, the beginning and the end
(22:13). He is who was, who is, who will be. We begin
because we find ourselves already born. We are forced, as
it were, to begin the game. This is the first grace. And
without the end, there is no game either. The game and
the song and the dance are one.

"When the gods play", Dag Hammarskjold wrote, "they
look for a string that has never been touched by man".[a]
No matter what note we seem to sound, a chord will be
discovered to bring it into harmony and melody attuned
to the rest of creation. We are to spend our lives sacrificing
and singing and dancing. There exists a *glory* that already
is. The universe exists because, as John says, "from his
fullness we have all received, grace upon grace" (Jn 1:16).
And this is my last point: *The spectator is not necessary
to the game, he merely beholds and cheers.*

The priest is the jester, the foolishness is the wisdom,
the missionary does come after the whisky. In our wildest
fantasy and imagination, we cannot conceive that we are
playing the most exciting game of all. The theology of play
merely means that our fantasies and our imaginations are
too small. To know this is true is to know both the most
difficult and the most glorious thing about being human,
about being what we are in the way we are.

NOTES

[1] Cf. Aristotle, *The Politics,* Chapter 8. Cf. J.V. Schall, *Play On:
From Games to Celebrations,* Philadelphia, Fortress, 1971.
[2] *Life on the Mississippi,* (1883), New York, Magnum, 1968,
p. 518.

[3] "The Priest and the Jester", *Dissent*, Spring, 1962, p. 233.
[4] *Life on the Mississippi*, p. 519.
[5] "Fern Hill", *Dylan Thomas: Selected Writings*, New Directions, 1946, p. 60.
[6] *Man, Play, and Games*, New York, The Free Press, 1961.
[7] *Affirmations of God and Man*, Association, 1967, p. x.
[8] *The Christian Universe*, Darton, 1966, p. 152.
[9] *Markings*, Knopf, 1964, p. 189.

Part IV

WHAT WE DO WHEN ALL ELSE IS DONE

Chapter XI

ON OFFICIALLY PRAYING

We are finite. We are fallen. We are in a vast universe in which we are offered glory and one another. We know we have a long history in which men and women have displayed every conceivable virtue and vice. So we know of our hypocrisy and our pride, that we are bored and that we hate too. Yet there are signs about that we are not locked into ourselves or even into our world. There is a loneliness in which we hear the laughter of creatures who are sad. We forgive and love our enemies because otherwise we go on and on in hatred and vengeance. And we play too. We discover that there are rules without which there is no game. And so we are fascinated by what is beyond us. What do we do when all else is done? This is a question that takes us back to the cathedrals built for praise, to men in search of glory. And the first thing we discover is that our praise and our prayer are our very response to our wonder that there is wonder at all.

When he promulgated the New Divine Office on the Feast of All Saints in 1970, Paul VI wrote:

> The Liturgy of the Hours gradually developed into the prayer of the local church, a prayer offered at regular intervals and in appointed places under the presidency of a priest. It was seen as a kind of necessary complement

J

to the fullness of divine worship that is contained in the eucharistic sacrifice, by means of which that worship might overflow to reach all the hours of daily life.

The notion of worship overflowing, reaching all the hours of our daily life is a moving one, for it is this worship and praise that we humorous men can give the Lord, something that serves to put all else in its order.

If we try to recall the image of the Roman Catholic priest, say, fifty or so years ago, then he was a man usually pictured walking about aimlessly in a biretta and cassock quietly mumbling words from the Breviary, an obviously ponderous tome said to be written in Latin, a language few people understood, including the average cleric, a task obviously consuming all the good man's free time. By the cynics the reading of the Divine Office (or Breviary) was clearly considered a heavy obligation, even a burden, the Catholic clergy's own little cross sort of a thing. It was said to be repetitious, even monotonous, a nearly fatal disease for a book.

As a reaction to all of this, however, Vatican II simplified the obligation of reading the Breviary (considered to be binding under serious sin in earlier ecclesiastical thinking) and recommended its renewal. Thus it became possible to substitute Scripture or other patristic or liturgical sources for it. Many in relief took advantage of this new attitude and dispensation.

The reformed Breviary

The Roman Catholic Church, however, is shrewder than we might give it credit for. In these days when no one will do anything unless it is *not* obligatory, the Church came up with a four volume Divine Office that is so good, so generally satisfying, that anyone, clergy or layperson, would be foolish to neglect it. These four volumes (to be read not at a sitting but throughout the year) are so refreshing, so surprising, that it is only with a sense of concrete loss that we fail to read a day in the year, or even an hour in the day. No treasury is quite so marvellous. It is indeed something broader than Christianity itself, almost the very best way to discover what it is that Christians believe in, how they look at God and the world and one another. I say this with some astonishment, since I would prefer to believe the Divine Office, or *The Liturgy of the Hours*, as it is now officially called, to be still a "burden", something onerous I could neglect rather than something profound and delightful that I simply miss if I do not pray it. But I find the new Liturgy of the Hours to be a complete pleasure and am reluctant to admit it even to myself.

The rhythm of the day

The very idea of the Liturgy of the Hours is a marvellous one — that the rhythm of each hour, each part of a day is different. Each day has its own character, each hour from sunrise to sunset and throughout the night has its own special mood as do the months and the seasons. And also we are only beginning to realize that the sense of season must appear differently for those on the Equator, where the sun sets promptly at six each night, and in the northern or southern hemispheres, where Christmas is either cold or hot, where the seasons are reversed. Each nation and clime must adapt something too.

Further, since the Old Testament and the time of Christ, Christians have been praying and living and singing their hymns so wonderfully found in the Office. They have been reading the Scriptures, the Psalms especially, reflecting on the sermons and writings of holy men and women before them. If the day be September 27th, for instance, it is the Feast of Vincent de Paul. I recall once several years ago being in Dax in South Western France, where Vincent was born. He seemed like such a small, simple saint to me at the time yet one of the major prophets of our modern concern about the poor.

The Breviary aids us in this remembering by giving us one of Vincent's sermons, in which he told us, sensibly:

> Do not become upset or feel guilty because you interrupted your prayer to serve the poor. God is not neglected if you leave him for such service. One of God's works is merely interrupted so that another can be carried out. So when you leave prayer to serve some poor person, remember that this very service is performed for God. Charity is certainly greater than any rule. Moreover, all rules lead to charity.

Any reasonably instructed Christian, of course, instinctively knows such a thing. Yet how refreshing it is to hear it from a St. Vincent, to realize that holy men maintained very sensible things, something we do not appreciate until we are confronted with their words and deeds. Often we do not know what we know — and it takes the whole tradition of Christianity to remind our dull hearts of beatitudes we cannot by ourselves suspect or comprehend.

And beyond all of this, we must be amazed — at least I was — to come across in the Poetry Section these remarkable "Lines written in her Breviary" of St. Teresa of Avila:

> Let nothing disturb thee,
> Nothing affright thee;
> All things are passing;
> God never changeth;
> Patient endurance
> Attaineth to all things;
> Who God possesseth
> In nothing is wanting;
> Alone God sufficeth.

So it is good to discover in the new Liturgy of the Hours not only Vincent and Teresa, Ecclesiastes, Jeremiah and the Psalms, Paul and James and Luke and Matthew, but also Polycarp, the *Imitation of Christ*, Augustine, Robert

Bellarmine, John XXIII, Leo the Great, the Venerable Bede, Ambrose, Clare of Assisi, Gregory the Great and Fulgentius, Elizabeth Ann Seton, Raymond of Penafort, Pius XI and Origen. How important it is for us to recognize that our generation is *not* the only one, that men from the second, seventh, thirteenth and nineteenth centuries also lived and worshipped the Lord. And how incredible really that these men can still speak to us if we will but listen.

Here we have much of our past riches organized for us according to a yearly and seasonal and daily rhythm and cycle. Morning prayers and evening prayers and afternoon prayers and night prayers, canticles and poems and hymns taken from so many diverse Christian sources, from Bach and the *Stralsund Gesangbuch,* from the *Cantionale Germanicum,* Old Gaelic and Welsh melodies, things we ought not to forget either. These are to be prayed and recited and sung by men and women who spend their lives slowly learning with Teresa that *God alone sufficeth.*

The Liturgy of the Hours makes the daily cycle; it increases our sensitivity to our very day. It reminds us that what we are about is a joy. The old monastic idea was that each hour of the day should find someone praising the Lord, just because the Lord is worthy of our praise. This is a moving and exalted sentiment. The second reading for Saturday of the Twenty-Fifth Week of the Year — the first is from Ezekiel — is from St. Hilary, Bishop. (Each day has a specific Scriptural reading plus a specific reading from one of the ancient, medieval, or modern sources of Christian reflection.) Hilary cited the Prophet in a sentence that has always been a favourite of mine: "There is a river whose streams gladden the City of God". Hilary went on to talk of the gifts of the Holy Spirit which "enter us like a gentle rain and once having done so, little by little, they bring forth fruit in abundance". It is well for us to remember that ancient bishops knew of the gentle rain and the river that gladdens the City of God, to remember this as we pass through our own days.

Such is our heritage from of old, that we can pray also as these men and women before us did. The Liturgy of the Hours is suddenly an unending, incredible treasure — meant for the clergy, I suppose. Yet I cannot but begin to feel that it is one of those wonderful things that are much too good for "Clerical use only". Indeed, the Divine Office has actually become one of those streams, those "rivulets", as another translation has it, that gladden the City of God. The burden, hopefully like all burdens eventually, has become a delight and a pleasure, something well worth discovering.

Yet am I being naïve to suggest that the Liturgy of the Hours can be used by everyone, not just for a few monks and sisters specially dedicated to reciting it in the legal name of us all?

Back in 1952, a British monk, Dom Illtyd Trethowan, wrote: "A lay person who 'says the Office' is a rarity in England, and is even regarded ... as a freak".[1] Over a decade after Vatican II, even monks and nuns who sing the daily Office are considered distinctly odd. I believe it fair to say that few people, be they lay or cleric, want their friends to consider them freakish or peculiar.

Is this the necessary conclusion, then, "Stay sane. Avoid the Divine Office"?

Not quite. I have pointed out that the Liturgy of the Hours is the official prayer of the Church. The word "official" should not throw us off. We should, I think, want the Church to guide us in our prayer and worship. We need to know how Christians pray and what they pray about. The Office is not the only way to pray, to be sure. The Church has always insisted on private and personal prayer also — meditation, reading, reflection, contemplation. Nor is the Liturgy of the Hours to be confused with or substituted for the Mass. Rather it attempts to organize each day, season and year in a way that some special worship and prayer is offered to the Lord fitting for the time and the place, something we pray knowing that other Christians in all places and languages pray as we do. This Divine Office comes out of our Jewish and Christian past to illuminate and consecrate our present.

Praying always

We were told in the New Testament to pray always and to ask for anything in Christ's name. The Liturgy of the Hours is the Church's effort to do exactly this. And this has always seemed impossible at first. But as we read, sing and reflect on the words and lessons that Christians of the past and today have used to pray this heritage, these hymns, psalms, petitions, readings, we know that we too can pray more than we know, we can realize that "always" begins in some small hour of a now, some place where we are.

The Church, then, does have a common prayer it wants us to know and love and be instructed by. Our very sharing these common days and seasons makes us talk the same language better, instructs us in the belief that we can only know it if we pray it, if we realize that we believe and pray in the Church, with our fellow Christians in whom the Spirit dwells among us. We are to be conscious of the meaning of our days and the course of our time. And we are to recognize that all life and time is "before" the Lord, before the Father to whom all praise, honour and glory are due, as the *Book of Revelation* recounts so beautifully. We are human persons who cannot and do not know themselves without praying to the Lord who has given them all they are.

Nonetheless, who wants to organize their days or their seasons? This sounds a bit rigid, even unromantic and impractical. Each week, however, a small guide is distributed to most homes in the modern world. Many eagerly buy it, few complain about it. In it, hour by hour, fifteen minutes by fifteen minutes, we are informed about what is to be on

153

television or radio. The content of the TV guide varies from season to season. Different kinds of programmes are arranged for morning and evening, for midnight, mid-afternoon, for late night shows even. Special occasions are listed apart from the regular routine — spectaculars, in-depth coverage, children's programmes. News recurrs periodically morning, noon and night. News commentators go on year after year like chant masters. In the autumn, we have football on Monday nights, on Saturdays and Sundays. New Year's Day in the United States has even become associated more and more with the Rose Bowl than making resolutions or even party-going. We have basket-ball, rugby, golf, cricket, tennis, motor-racing and baseball in their seasons. The Olympics have become something of a special event. And every four years also, we have presidential conventions and elections in the United States and every country gives its political life a regular coverage.

While these various programmes are actually on the air, they all are interspersed, especially in the United States but all countries have their forms of interruptions, every five or ten or fifteen or thirty minutes with highly developed, to-the-point advertisement or announcements, repeated over and over so that they often become quite familiar. We can sing the Schlitz Beer commercial back, and we recite the virtues of the latest model Chevrolet or Bentley or aspirin tablet with ease. Favourite comedians like Archie Bunker or Bill Cosby reappear week after week at the same time. Many of us are there regularly to watch these or other familiar programmes of our taste. And now there are elaborate recording devices to replay what we missed so that while we may neglect to pray, we need not miss our favourite programmes.

Anyone who watches television all day and night is a "freak", "peculiar". Yet most people watch it quite a bit of the time, at regular intervals, gazing at the recurring advertisements, programmes and schedules. Such people are quite normal. Most of us belong to the group.

Now in a real sense the Church and the monks invented

this way of organizing and ordering the days and the seasons, the hours even. This is nothing other than the Divine Office method itself. The difference is one of media and content, but the essential structure and discipline are not all that different when we come to think of it. All sorts of secularized Christian practices lie about and we fail to recognize them or retranslate them into our religious life.

Both complex and simple

Nonetheless, why should anyone give up television for the Office? First of all, I think, we probably need at least one radio and television system on which we can attempt to present and develop the Liturgy of the Hours for the media everybody watches or listens to anyhow. I am not at all sure it could not even compete. Were our values right, the Liturgy of the Hours and television are in a way made for each other. It says something for our own lack of real freedom of religion and our disunity, as well as our lack of enterprise, that we do not think more in these terms, though I saw a One-Minute Spot TV recently put out by the Franciscans on one of the Psalms that showed what might be done. Television and radio can remind us and educate us, reach us in our own homes and offices and cars, in our very privacy. Still, the best place for praying and worshipping is in the parish, the monastery, the chapel, the home, even in our room.

The layperson or the cleric or the sister who recites or sings the Liturgy of the Hours daily and regularly is no more freakish or singular than the same person who watches or listen to television or radio for a definite time each day or week. So let us put this one myth aside for good.

Yet it is still legitimate to wonder if the money we spend for the four volume Liturgy of the Hours is suitable and profitable expenditure for the average layperson. There is considerable controversy over this question that should not be ignored. Many think the new Divine Office is too complex and unwieldly even yet, aimed at the professionals, not at everyone, too long, too scholarly, too technical.

Nevertheless, the Liturgy of the Hours ought not to be all confusion. And it is not. It is very compact; its repetitions and its rhythms are suited to our human way of knowing. Anyone who is interested in the Office should read carefully Paul VI's brief Promulgation Message and the more thorough General Instruction found in Volume One of the New Breviary. Further, by thumbing and asking and trying it out to learn our way about the Liturgy of the Hours, we will gradually become familiar with it. The best way to do this is simply to find and read everything properly belonging to a given day from start to finish, so that the "geography" of the Office will be seen. It will appear a bit chaotic at first, but this is normal. Each year too, publishers and translators usually will put out a brief summary guide to each day's readings.

For monks and for everyone else

The essential parts of the Liturgy of the Hours are the Morning and Evening Prayers. These consist in Scriptural readings, followed by special prayers. There will be readings from Christian sources about the saint or nature of the day. The other prayers for midday or night or afternoon are intended to be brief and read when convenient during that time. The best approach is simply to find where each day's readings are and to read various parts gradually according to available time and interest. Something will always be meaningful and prayerful in each day's readings. For most people it is enough to concentrate on these. This mode of reading is for our own private day, its schedule and needs.

The Liturgy of the Hours, however, can and should be at one time or another said or sung in a larger group where its riches are more publicly manifest. Professor William Storey has worried that the present Office is still not designed for practical use in the average parish where some short, familiar form of morning and evening song ought to be recited or sung.[2] The Liturgy of the Hours should be a public thing also. This means that our parishes, universities, monasteries and schools should practice and teach us how better to pray these Hours by example and instruction. Indeed, I believe we need several core instruction groups composed of well-trained and sympathetic teachers to come about periodically in cities and parishes to give us pilot possibilities on how to use the Office simply and meaningfully. If it takes ten or twenty years to begin as a nation, this is quite all right in the long run.

All share the same reason for rejoicing

No one, then, wants to make monks out of lay persons. Some of our monks should sing the Office in its completeness. We need this too. There is no reason why there cannot be a perfectly valid use of the Liturgy of the Hours for full exposition in monasteries and episcopal cathedrals, adapted and varied smaller versions for parishes, more familiar ones for families and quite flexible readings for individuals. We live in a literate and inventive society. It seems ridiculous to admit that the millions of educated Catholics in the English-speaking world cannot learn to read and sing the parts of the Office according to their own needs and inclinations.

The Liturgy of the Hours is to be prayed by ourselves, with our families on occasion, by our parishes and in our cloisters. Each bishop, I think, owes it to us to have at least some place in his diocese in which we can learn and see how the Divine Office might be well used for the worship of God. The Liturgy of the Hours ought not to be "forced" upon us. That is not its point or spirit. The worship of God is something that we want to do, something that we will do when we realize its beauty and power. But still we need to be reminded to pray, and to pray the way the Church officially does.

There is, I think, a final thing that we must realize about our faith that the Liturgy of the Hours will teach us, if we will let it. It is this: after all, it is God whom we worship in whatever worldly condition or mood we find ourselves in. The Christian tradition that we are handed in these Hours constantly reminds us that God alone is worthy of praise and worship. If we forget this, we cut ourselves off from the end of our beginning. The major difficulty, even heresy, of our time is undoubtedly the gradual substitution of humanity or man for God as the object of our worship and concern. It is astonishing how the Office never wavers here, how it keeps its eyes firmly planted on the object of praise and adoration.

To conclude, let me cite two random passages from the Liturgy of the Hours that bring us back to what our daily, hourly praise is about. The first is from the Second Reading of Christmas Day, taken from a Sermon of St. Leo the Great, Pope:

Dearly Beloved, today our Saviour is born; let us rejoice. Sadness should have no place on the birthday of life. The fear of death has been swallowed up; life brings us joy with the promise of eternal happiness. No one is shut out from this joy; all share the same reason for rejoicing. Our Lord, victor over sin and death, finding no man free from sin, came to free us all.

The second passage is from St. Columban, Abbot, from his Instruction found on his Feast on November 23:

Moses wrote in the Law: *God made man in his image and likeness.* Consider, I ask you, the dignity of these words. God is all-powerful. We cannot see or understand him, describe or assess him. Yet he fashioned man from clay and endowed him with the nobility of his own image. What has man in common with God? Or earth with spirit? — *for God is a spirit.* It is a glorious privilege that God should grant man his eternal image and the likeness of his character. Man's likeness to God, if he preserves it, imparts high dignity.

158

The Liturgy of the Hours keeps us constantly before what we are and what God is. This is the mystery which Christianity for two thousand years has maintained. It is also our hope and our joy. We can, in short, pray always. We fallen, finite men and women can worship God. The need and the desire to do so is everywhere about us. We all share the same reason for rejoicing. Our Lord, finding no man free from sin, came to free us all. Consider, I ask you, the dignity of these words that *God* made man in his image and likeness. Whom God possesseth, in nothing is wanting. *God alone sufficeth.*

NOTES

[1] *Christ in the Liturgy,* p. 120.
[2] Cf. "Parish Worship: The Liturgy of the Hours", *Worship,* January, 1975; "The Liturgy of the Hours: Cathedral Versus Monastery", *Worship,* January, 1976.

Chapter XII

ON THE UNIVERSITY, THE MONASTERY
AND THE CITY

And if God alone sufficeth, as Teresa of Avila taught us, if we have a worship of prayer, if we are to sacrifice and sing and dance before the Lord, build cathedrals rather than tear them down, knowing that we are made in God's image even in our bodies somehow, what do we do when all else is done? Are we but tools to another age or generation? Yet we cannot be, we are already persons in whom the full justification for our existence already exists. What then do we need to know about the purpose of our basic institutions, especially about our universities, our monasteries and our cities?

The road to Monte Cassino winds upward steeply amidst rather barren rocks, stone fences, olive groves, ever drawing away from the valley below through which a good part of Western civilization has at one time or another passed. When I finally made it up to Monte Cassino one spring, I realized that here was where mankind first began to realize that work was not a curse but could be freely chosen, shared among the brothers.[1] *Ora et Labora*, work and pray, this I remembered was the great Benedictine motto. Here too was where men began to realize that organization and discipline were enormously productive even when they were meant merely to assist at prayer.

And it was here also that the notion of the Platonic guardians began to take on its peculiarly Christian configuration, where poverty, chastity and obedience replaced common wives and children, where praise of the Lord replaced the contemplation of the good. "The monastery was in fact", Lewis Munford wrote in *The City of History,*

> a new kind of polis: an association, or rather, a close brotherhood of like-minded people, not coming together for occasional ceremonies, but for permanent cohabitation, in an effort to achieve on earth a Christian life, addressed solely and single-mindedly to the service of God . . . The closest link between the classic city and the medieval city was that formed, then, not by the surviving buildings and customs, but by the monastery.[2]

The monastery, then, is an essential part of our very civil tradition.

Another essential part of the medieval city was the university. The justification for the university which our culture has received from this tradition is that the university exists to provide a place where knowledge and truth could be sought in a human way, sought not because they were relevant, or pertinent, or politically significant, but simply (to use a Greek notion) for their own sakes. Thus, the study of the Latin tongue or of aorist participles, or Hindu myths, or God Almighty, need no further justification than the fact that they exist and are in themselves intrinsically fascinating.

Professor Bruce Park once wrote a remarkable essay relating in a way, the university and the city.[3] Part of the trouble, he implied, is that today the very nature of the social sciences themselves, whose popularity has been evident but whose method and philosophical justification have deprived them of anything but the "now" as a subject matter, is in question. Indeed, even literature and the natural sciences fall under the merciless scrutiny of the "now" — the dominance of the latest movement and moods. It is not without interest that English professors and nuclear scientists have come forth in recent decades as the voices of contemporary politicizing movements in the universities. But, as many perceptive critics of the contemporary scene more and more come to discover, the exclusive study of the now — current movements and values — is an essentially backward and conservative enterprise. What is needed, Professor Park suggested, is contemplation and distance.

Universities must again enter an academic plane where people can think. This does not mean areas of free debate. Much that goes on by that name is the weary, embittered exchange of slogans and cliches. But slogans, cliches and fears aside, debate, free or not, has little to do with whether men find it possible to reflect. Debate is a poor relation to thought, however valuable it may be to lawyers and legislators.

The need for the monastery is discernible in several quarters on the campus . . . Students . . . are becoming anxious to escape the hubbub of other motives, other ends, other actions into a place where they can think.

Now, a place in which to "think" is not yet a monastery, perhaps, but it is the beginning of one. What is remarkable, however, is that the need of the monastery becomes most evident precisely when the university becomes most politicized.

A place to pray and worship

A monastery is essentially a place to pray and worship. In Western tradition, formal political speculation, that is, thought about the city, began with the search for a thinker, a philosopher king who could truly know the absolute good and thereby share it with all men in the polis. The Christian monastery, as conceived by the early

Benedictines, believed that the worship of God and the fraternity of the brothers were prerequisites to knowledge. For the Greeks, action led to contemplation. For the Christian, thought was the natural overflow of prayer and worship. *Credo ut intelligam* — I believe in order to understand. But for both, the pursuit of knowledge could not be divorced from the ultimate questions.

Thus I have the impression today that the simultaneous socialization of academic and cultural life along with a feeling that intellectual integrity often requires a fleeing from this very world is somewhat a consequence of our refusal to acknowledge that worship is an essential element in the pursuit of truth. What has been missing has been precisely a sense of the whole. The politicization of literature, science and knowledge is really the creation of a substitute whole, the denial that there is any fundamental distinction between religion and politics.

What has in fact happened has been the working out of the idea that man, not God, is the highest being, that a kind of politics is all there is. Yet the spectre of Augustine's "Our hearts are restless until they rest in Thee" still hangs over our culture in spite of all our efforts to exorcise it. The monastery again begins to cast its shadow on the world though the building itself is perhaps nowhere yet to be seen.

Several years ago I was in Venice. On the way to somewhere in that marvellous city (I forget where now, because like San Francisco, Rome, or Bruges, everywhere you go in Venice seems more astonishing than the place you just left) I came across the house where Marco Polo lived. I was reminded of this when I later chanced to buy a book of early travellers' tales which contained an account of Marco Polo's first meeting with Kublai Khan, "The Lord of the Tartars all over the earth", as he put it. Kublai Khan had never seen a "Latin" before so he was anxious to meet one. After hearing a description of this strange part of the world, the Tartar King decided to send a goodwill mission to see the Pope. He asked the Pope to send some

K

hundred Christian men to his court. In Polo's account, they were to be

> intelligent men, acquainted with the seven arts, well qualified to enter into controversy and able to prove clearly by force of argument to idolators and other kind of folk, that the Law of Christ was best, and that all other religions were false and naught; and that if they could prove this, he and all under him would become Christians and the Church's liegemen.[4]

Of course, it is not my purpose here to "prove by the force of argument to idolaters and other kind of folk that the law of Christ is best", though I would hope that all of us could have some of the famous Mongol warrior's intellectual humility and openness. What I wish to suggest, however, is that the crisis of the university and the city does relate directly to the neglect of that element of religion and cultural life that has been protected and fostered in the monastery.

The new centre of involvement

Behind all of these issues of the relation of our culture to the monastery and the university and the city lies the relation between prayer and politics. This is the classical problem of the relation of action and contemplation as it exists in our own world. My initial conclusions are these: modern social and political movements, be they anti-war, ecological, or Third World development, have so identified religion and spirituality with their this-worldly programmes that they are in grave danger of losing their religious foundation and justification which is the transcendence and mystery of God.

The need and longing for the monastery in the modern world, therefore, is a sign of a rejection of the greatest heresy Christian theory can conceive, namely the direct identification of the divine purpose with the this-worldly affairs of men. Dom Odo Brooke, in his reflective essay,

"The Monk and the World", wrote that the essential question is not an either/or alternative of immersing oneself in or fleeing from the affairs of the world as if this were the only alternative. "Our involvement in the world is not partial but total. But we (monks) are involved in the world from a new centre which not partially but totally transcends the world. We are therefore engaged totally in the world from a centre totally beyond the world".[5] It is this lack of attention to the transcendent centre that constitutes the essential political problem of our time. Mumford was right: You cannot build the complete city without the Abbey church.

All this will seem, undoubtedly, unsettling and even obscure, though it is my view that it flows directly from the evolution of political theory in the modern world. In order to understand why this is so, let me begin by citing two other Englishmen, both of whom have always been somehow symbols of sanity to me. These are the great Anglican theologian Eric Mascall and the justly famous storyteller, J.R.R. Tolkien. In his perceptive review of J.B. Metz's *The Theology of the World*, Mascall pointed out the danger of the effort to transform theology into politics, no matter how much partial truth it might contain. He wrote:

> Finally, without in the least degree questioning Father Metz's concern with secularization and technology, I would suggest that the Christian theologian ought not to commit himself too confidently to an identification of the future with a theology that is developed in terms of our technological culture. I would ask the question . . . whether the future of Christianity and the Church may not lie with the peoples of Asia and Africa, for whom even the terrific impact of western secularity does not seem to have destroyed a sense of the divine transcendence.[6]

European theologians, to be sure, tend to overstress both technology and the contemplative traditions of the Third

World. In any case, the sense of the transcendent at the core of political thought is still the basic question because the ultimate check on all politics is precisely the validity of the contemplative order.

The second aspect I should like to stress is the fact that man already is a special being of some wholly improbable sort in the universe. Tolkien put it well:

> Supernatural is a dangerous and difficult word in any of its senses, looser or stricter. But to fairies it can hardly be applied, unless super is taken merely as a superlative prefix. For it is man who is, in contrast to fairies, supernatural (and often of diminutive stature); whereas they are natural, far more natural than he. Such is their doom.[7]

What Tolkien realized is that the metaphysical status of man is, as it were, in a category apart because man is a creature in the universe directly invited to contemplate the divine. Christianity means precisely the invitation to share the proper internal life of the trinitarian God. There is no worldly political substitute for this, nor can there be. This is why the one essential thing the totalitarian or secular mind must suppress is the contemplative.

Simply centred on God

Not so long ago, I chanced on an older essay of Watkin Williams on "The Statecraft of St Bernard of Clairvaux" in the old *Dublin Review*.

> The Church, St Bernard would have contended, is ruled as are the angels and, in his ideology, the State is also theocracy. Before the angels were confirmed in their allegiance, some of them fell. Man as an individual remains, during his earthly lifetime, still on probation. As a corporation, the ultimate destiny of the Church as an Ecclesia Triumphans is divinely assured. As a corporation, no state has any ultimate destiny at all. Its individual

citizens, whether rulers or ruled, have such a destiny submitted to their free choice, but only as citizens, actual or possible, of the City of God. In this sense, we may interpret the statecraft of St Bernard. It simply centred on God, to whom every measure taken by the civil ruler should be referred.[8]

For the mystical Doctor, this "supernaturalness" of man, this ultimate City of God was his true home. Individual men could not, politically, forget it. It is to this reality that the contemplative in human society stands as abiding witness.

Yet the question arises naturally, particularly with the oppressing problems of social action and Marxist-eschatological theology, whether this emphasis on the other life does not simply lay the Christian open to the charge of abandoning the world of man to itself. Moreover, for contemporary Marxist theologians, political theology is directly the building of a "heaven", indeed the building of the ultimate heaven. For the non-Christian, this heaven is on earth, the elimination of all intrinsic and extrinsic alienation. For the Christian, it is one of the basic continuity between what man does and what God does. But in any Christian view, heaven is God's work.

Prayer and politics

The two opposing extremes of Christian analysis, the complete activist and the total contemplative as they appear in the contemporary world, raise issues that cannot be avoided. In my own thinking, I am inclined to the view that it is the contemplative that is today the most neglected and the most important. This runs the danger of standing aloof from much recent Christian political activity, especially Third World and radical social action theory, which tend to identify social and political activity with the faith. Further, the twenty-fifth chapter of Matthew, the Epistle of James, the books of Amos and Isaiah must always remain a fundamental part of any relationship to God. And these parts of Scripture are strongly social action warnings. Yet my view here is that the monastery in particular and the contemplative life in general are at present the most required things in the specifically modern world because what is required is the realization that political action and economic productivity, necessary though they be, are not the essence of the faith or man.

In recent years, two remarkable essays have been written upon the relation of politics and prayer by French theologians, the late Jean Daniélou's "Prayer as a Political Problem" and Jacques Ellul's "Prayer and Modern Man". Daniélou's approach was through the public order. Prayer, he held, requires a civilizational context which it is not receiving. This cuts the common man off from a sense of the sacred and divine. He greatly feared that Christianity might become merely a cult of the élite. Politics is not mysticism or sanctity. But it does exist to make such things possible so that without this openness to the holy, the sacred invades politics — a phenomenon that is currently happening everywhere in the Western world. But it is a holiness that is warped and exaggerated precisely because it is not recognized as such.

"A city which does not possess churches as well as factories", Daniélou continued,

> is not fit for men. It is inhuman. The task of politics is to assure to men a city in which it will be possible for them to fulfill themselves completely, to have a full material, fraternal and spiritual life. It is for this reason that in so far as it expresses this personal fulfilment of man in a particular dimension, prayer is a political problem; for a city which would make prayer impossible would fail in its role as a city.[9]

The very nature of contemporary civilization requires the moment of personal prayer both to establish the absolute dignity of the individual and to set limits to civilization itself. The philosophic, ecological and political movements to return man to a generalized species instead of a person are already far advanced. Politics can and must demand of religion, in its turn, that its prayer be real and vital. The Christian notion of Cæsar and God, however, must remain the essential foundation of the priority and relationship of man to the state.

Ellul's approach to prayer and politics is almost the very opposite of Daniélou's. "Why do men not pray?" he asked. The main reason seems to be that Christianity has come to be looked upon as a kind of service, an aid-giving brotherhood whose religious meaning and task are totally exhausted in such efforts. Modern technique has supposedly been able to do everything that God used to be called upon to do. Thus the mission of religion is merely a kind of supplemental distribution, concern-arousing agency.

For Ellul, political action, no matter how radical, is still in this world. It must always belong to the condition of time. Politics is of itself never God or God-producing. "Prayer, by contrast, is a much more radical break, a more fundamental protest", he wrote in *Prayer and Modern Man*. "Precisely because our technological society is given over to action, the person who retires to his room to prayer is the true radical".[10] Prayer is thus seen as combat, as the positive effort to create precisely history, to save our deeds from meaninglessness. The Incarnation is still present as an active power in the world, a judgment of men and nations. The true order of history is a salvation history. Aside from this, all political action is only itself. It has no order intrinsic to it nor any interior meaning. Where the Marxist finds absolute continuity and competence, Ellul finds only faith and interruption.

The contact of play, joy and politics

Religion in general and Christianity in particular are not to be judged or justified primarily by their political consequences or lack thereof. The First Commandment is always, "Thou shalt love the Lord thy God". There is a type of Christian thought, C.S. Lewis wrote in his very stimulating little book, *Letters to Malcolm, Chiefly Concerning Prayer,* which seeks to save Christianity by removing the supernatural from it to make it, supposedly, more acceptable to modern man. But this, of course, is exactly what modern man does not need. What he needs is, in a very real sense, what is beyond need. It is the failure to acknowledge this basic aspect of man that is currently challenging both the university and the city.

Essentially, then, what I have been trying to say in this regard is that what the monastery stand for, the worship of God, the pursuit of truth, the love of the brotherhood, is what the city and the university must regain. I do not mean that the city and the university must become the monastery (a temptation the China of Mao seemed to have succumbed to in a secular form) but they must feel its presence within their very legitimate realities. What new or old communal form this will take I am not at all sure. I am beginning to feel that the future of the Christian family absolutely needs some kind of communal form if we are to preserve its values and vigour into the next century. This may also be true of the very history and recollection of what man is.

We need to realize further that prayer is the first and most radical political act because it establishes who we are in the course of cosmic history, while it limits politics to this world. Prayer, then, is the basic breaking out of the confinement of human persons within their world and their times.

But this breaking out is, as it were, essentially an astonishment. As Tolkien said, it is man who is the real supernatural being in the universe. Elves and trolls and hobbits are natural. This means that the sorrows and tasks of the world are not meant to be final or to distract us from our ultimate business. But in a way, even for us our supernatural status can also be "our doom" like that of the natural creatures. We are really free, to repeat, to reject our own good and the triune life of God that we are promised. This is the ultimate drama in all political societies.

For the Greeks, nevertheless, the final condition of man on earth was to be leisure. Christianity did not reject this view but said that leisure was not merely the end of politics — the place where prayer and contemplation could naturally happen — but also, in a way, it was also the life of God to which man is invited. C.S. Lewis put it well:

> Dance and game are frivolous, unimportant down here; for 'down here' is not their natural place. Here they are moment's rest from the life we were placed here to live. But in this world everything is upside-down. That which, if it could be prolonged here, would be truancy, is likest that which in a better country is the End of ends. Joy is the serious business of heaven.[11]

The contemplative life as it was historically called is, then, our greatest and most immediate political and intellectual need. This is the paradox within the religious politics of our time.

So it is that the existence and vitality of this higher life, our constant realization of its presence, is what keeps us open to that true dignity that belongs to us as men, the dignity that we actually were called to accept and share the life of God. The political history of recent centuries, and more especially of recent years, it seems to me, is little else than the search, in its theoretical depths, for a viable alternative to this gift. Ultimately it is the person who performs the trans-political acts of prayer, worship and praise. He is the one who knows that all proposed alternatives (alternatives he is obliged to know and understand because he too has the gift of intelligence) are of lesser dignity. This is why prayer and praise are really the only valid revolutionary acts in the modern world.

For they alone "turn around" worldly conditions and escape from their limits.

The shadow of Monte Cassino is still somehow in the world, in our cities and in our universities. The reason it will not go away is very theological and very political. It is, as Tolkien said, because man is the supernatural creature, the only one with a touch of *glory*. At last, he is the one for whom joy is the serious business to which he is called.

NOTES

[1]Cf. L. Mumford's *Technics and Civilization*.
[2] Harcourt, Brace, 1961.
[3] "Give Me Back My Ivory Tower", *National Observer*, 29 September 1971.
[4] *Traveller's Tales*, ed. J. du Bois, New York, Everyman's Vacation Publications, nd.
[5] *The Downside Review*, April, 1970.
[6] Mascall, *The Downside Review*, April, 1970.
[7] "On Fairy Stories", *The Tolkien Reader*, Ballantine, 1968.
[8] *The Dublin Review*, April, 1943.
[9] *Prayer as a Political Problem*, trans., J. Kirwan, New York, Sheed, 1967.
[10] *Prayer and Modern Man*, Seabury, 1970.
[11] *Letters to Malcolm*, New York, Harcourt, 1964.

Chapter XIII

ON WORSHIP

Prayer and play, politics and contemplation, fallenness and glory: such realities are bound together in ways we might not have expected had we not tried to wonder if Christianity just might not be true, after all. Our sense of doom is strong, yet it often seems but the other side of salvation, of our destiny for joy, since there are some things we can only have if we choose to have them even though they be true gifts. We have touched often on the glory and the wisdom that transcend our lot. The praise of fallen men, then, is a worship of God. So it is well now to take a look at worship. For it is the highest thing we do when all else is done.

And I should like to begin by citing the famous nineteenth century Russian Orthodox writer, Nicholas Gogol, in his *Méditations sur la Divine Liturgie,* a dusty old book I found last year up in the library of the Jesuit Villa above Frascati. I do not want merely to recall that men of other ages and cultures praised the Lord in Office and Liturgy, but also I want to note how Gogol reminded us that worship of the Lord is what keeps us from hatred too, that worship does have a place even in our cities, our centres of learning, our very civilization.

The Divine Liturgy is the eternal recommencement of the sublime act of love accomplished for us . . . This is why whoever wishes to progress and to become better ought to attend as often as possible the divine liturgy and listen to it with attention: for it builds and fashions man imperceptibly. And if society is not yet corrupted completely, if among men we do not yet breathe a total, implacable hatred, the profound reason for it returns to the divine liturgy which recalls to man that holy and celestial love for his brother.[1]

This is a powerful passage. It recalls to us again that the "sublime act of love" begins ever anew among even us — doomed, fallen, supernatural creatures that we are. It recalls too that we must keep straight our thinking on our friendships with God and with one another.

There is often a certain confusion between friendship and liturgy that is of some importance to clarify, something that gives me occasion for remark because of the Byzantine rite to which Gogol belonged. I often suspect that the ancients were fundamentally right when they distinguished carefully between friendliness, comradeship and friendship, when they said that we would not have more than two or three real friends in our whole lives. Some would see this as a rather pessimistic thing. But I am inclined to think rather that friendship was seen as such a deep and lasting thing that life is not long enough to have so many. Nor need it be.

The Eucharist, no doubt, is a "friendship-forming" and "friendship-expressing" celebration. It is where the Lord first called us friends. But the liturgy is primarily worship, the place, the action, as it were, in which we are more concerned with the First Commandment than we are with the Second. In the liturgy, our immediate focus is the Father, the Son, the Spirit; the God who created us too by an infinite "word" that makes us to be only ourselves and no one else; whose redemption touched us according to our own names, in our own histories and lives. Friendship is a mystery because personhood is a mystery.

Thomas Merton said something that I think is very

wise, that is very pertinent to our worship and our relationship to one another.

Do not stress too much the fact that love seeks to penetrate the intimate secrets of the beloved. Those who are too fond of this idea fall short of true love, because they violate the solitude of those they love, instead of respecting it . . .

A person is a person insofar as he has a secret and is a solitude of his own that cannot be communicated to anyone else . . .

Our failure to respect the intimate spiritual privacy of other persons reflects a secret contempt for God himself . . .

It is at once our loneliness and our dignity to have an incommunicable personality that is ours, ours alone and no one else's, and will be so forever . . .

If I cannot distinguish myself from the mass of other men, I will never be able to love and respect other men as I ought.[2]

This brings us back, of course, to loneliness and silence as a beginning of the discovery of ourselves and of God; to the realization that we are already persons, mysteries created in our own uniqueness for the choice to love the triune God, and this forever. The fellowship of worship, then, must retain, indeed foster, this sense that the man or woman next to us is precisely "at prayer" in liturgy, that the direction of the communication is not towards us, even though we too are all enveloped in the reality that allows us to acknowledge the God who is not ourselves.

Thus I have need in a very deep sense of my neighbour's worship, of the sense that the person next to me transcends, as do all persons, even the social order of all of us; that each worshipping person at prayer belongs first to God and that, unless he does, he cannot belong to me. The love of friendship (that extraordinary experience which can begin in a moment, but which usually takes the time to know character, value and orientation) is soon exhausted if we create ourselves and one another, if we are "responsible" totally for what the other is. What fascinates us most about our friends is precisely that inexhaustible surprise we discover in them, that wondrous realization that the true depth of other persons is somehow beyond all human measure.

To be deprived of what we do not yet have

Jacques Maritain in a memorable chapter remarked that " . . . What makes man most unhappy is to be deprived, not of that which he had, but of that which he did not have, and did not really know".[3] These remarks are from a reflection on love and friendship. And what we shall be deprived of is the inner life and love of most people who have ever lived. We ultimately share in the mystery of very few persons during our years among the human lot. And this is true (this is, in fact, Maritain's point) because the richness of creation is beyond what we can ever ourselves comprehend in one lifetime. That others know what we cannot and will not is the great blessing of the mystery of friendship. The claim to immediate friendship, the claim that all our thoughts and feelings and loves ought to be open to everyone else, is a subtle form of private totalitarianism. This is why Aristotle once held, and all totalitarian rulers since have practiced, that there can be no real friendship allowed in a tyranny, nothing of a personal and private nature; that there be no secrets known to one that are not known to all.

The worship of the Father through the Son in the Spirit is the means by which we can be content that our neighbour can be left to himself in his own loves and happinesses, which shall not be ours. We must be content that God loves each person differently, that each friendship contains a mystery that cannot be public. But that is the negative side of it. The positive side, as it were, is that even the hope of fulfillment for any human friendship cannot be founded on the friendship itself but only in worship where each one is aware that the person who is our friend loves God first. In this is our peace and our humility.

Evil and worship

Alexander Schmemann, in his remarkable analysis of Solzhenitsyn, noted that the great Russian writer possesses intrinsically the three Christian attitudes that constitute Christianity's essential outlook: 1) the belief that the world really is created by God, that it is good in itself; 2) the belief that men have in fact fallen; 3) the belief that they are redeemed. Solzhenitsyn is the one major figure in the world today who insists that all evil is through persons and that it demands sorrow; that political reforms or economic ones are not enough; that, in short, the first words of Mark's Gospel are still the first ones to accomplish for changing the world.

Evil in Solzhenitsyn is real because it is always personal. It does not lie in an impersonal system, nor does it come from impersonal structures. It is ever in men and through the means of men. Evil is always and first of all constituted by evil men, men who have chosen and who constantly choose evil, men who effectively have chosen to serve it. And therefore, evil in every case is a fall, every time a choice. . . .

Meanwhile, the incubus of evil consists in the fact that living, concrete, personal men torment other men and above all in the fact that they would be able, if they should wish it, not to torment them. But this is the Christian intuition of evil. . . . In Solzhenitsyn, evil remains always in the sphere of morality, and consequently of the personal. It is always referred to that consciousness that is given to me.[4]

177

This sense of the locus and reality of evil in the world is directly connected with our worship of God. For the status of evil, as it were, is not to be judged in terms other than those of personal choice.

And so it is, behind all the movements, structures and ideologies which seek to explain our dire lot in another way lies the firm, unyielding insistence that persons choose; that the drama of their choice is the drama of history; that God is related to us directly in this power of choosing, in loving him and in rejecting him. And it is in the violation of our brother that we see the consequences of our failure to worship God who made our brother also. Quite literally, God allows no other worship but of himself. Paradoxically, this is the only way we can be secure in what we are as men, secure indeed and safe from other worshippers who find no absolute in their neighbour.

The simple truth

That Christianity retained this essence of itself, then, is of the utmost importance. "For many reasons we have need of Christianity", Laszak Kolakowski has observed,

> but not of just any sort of Christianity. We have no need of a Christianity which makes political revolutions, which hastens to cooperate in the so-called sexual liberation, which would approve our concupiscence and exalt our violence. There are already sufficient forces in the world for all that without the aid of Christianity.
>
> Men have need of a Christianity which aids them in going beyond their difficulties of life, which gives them awareness of the fundamental limits of the human condition and a capacity to accept them, of a Christianity which teaches them that simple truth not only is there a tomorrow but a beyond tomorrow, and that the difference between success and defeat is rarely discernible.[5]

But if Christianity is to retain this essence of itself, if it is not to be transformed into a pale imitation of the contemporary ideologies or psychologies which seek to root all reality in man and his world, then we must tenaciously hold to the certitude of worship in our personal lives.

When he began his famous walk, Hilaire Belloc wrote some lines about our need to begin the day with Mass. His reasons were very worldly ones, that is, ones very close to the kind of physical, waffling beings we often are. There is a sort of physical pleasure and contentment in beginning the day with a Mass which Belloc found comforting, whatever the theologians might have said about it. And for these comforts, Belloc perceived four causes which are well worth considering again some seventy-five years after he formulated them:

1. That for half-an-hour just at the opening of the day you are silent and recollected, and have to put off cares, interests and passions in the repetition of a familiar action. This must certainly be a great benefit to the body and give it tone.

2. That the Mass is a careful and rapid ritual. Now it is the function of all ritual (as we see in games, social arrangements and so forth) to relieve the mind by so much of responsibility and initiative and to catch you up (as it were) into itself, leading your life for you during the time it lasts. . . .

3. That the surroundings incline you to good and reasonable thoughts, and for the moment deaden the rasp and jar of that busy wickedness which both working in one's self and received from others is the true source of all human miseries. . . .

4. And the most important cause of this feeling of satisfaction is that you are doing what the human race has done for thousands upon thousands upon thousands of years.[6]

Belloc, of course, knew and loved the short Masses of the Latin rite. He once remarked that this brief rite was among the greatest of human spiritual inventions, the one

L

that was most attuned to the way most men are, which protected them from the excessively spiritual out of which so many difficulties arise, much more than from the flesh. The sense of recollection, the being carried away in an action that draws us out, the awareness of our faults and wickedness, the sense of sharing in the history of our race — such too are parts of our worship. Without our active energies and efforts to make our personhood aware of these, we become less than we are meant to be.

The worship of God, not neighbour

We are used to distinguishing public and private worship. We are aware that liturgy can lead to or be a contemplation. We know too that even in action we can reach a kind of contemplation, as Ignatius of Loyola taught. But whatever the approach, it remains important that the contemplation and worship of God be the central act of each person. This is the result of the spiritual depth that already exists within each human being on account of what he is from his beginning and over which he has no control. We are born already men. We do not "make" ourselves so, as so many would seem to pretend. This means that we cannot neglect that aspect of our faith, indeed its central tenet, that it is God alone whom we worship.

René Voillaume, in a remarkable passage, has written:

It is true that what we do to the least of our brothers we do to God and no one knows how to love God if he does not love his fellows. Therefore, we speak of the same direction of our love. This, nonetheless, is directed to two objects, since God remains distinct from our brothers and deserves to be loved for himself. Christ lives in the heart of every man but that which I touch in my brothers is not God in person, nor Christ, but his image, the presence of his grace. . . .

But to be content to search for God by loving our

brothers and commending ourselves generously to them, is this not to remain in some way imprisoned within the limits of our humanity? . . . Are we reduced to contemplating the works of the Lord and are we not able to contemplate the Lord himself in a direct way? I would dare to say in this point that a Christian who no longer would concern himself to contemplate the Lord Jesus and to love him above all things, would not be able, whatever be the generosity of his gift to the service of man, to love them as Jesus had taught him.[7]

The sense that worship, private and public, ought to remain our primary act as free men is beginning to take on a new significance. There is a danger that the opium of the people will not any longer be "religion" but rather the very belief that somehow we can satisfy men with the world. If we go to our churches and find nothing more than we find in our newspapers and our sociology books and in our group therapy units, we will, if we are wise, cease going to church.

Men who worship ought to know about the condition of men about them, to be sure. Their worship is also legitimately and necessarily petition for one another, as the Lord's Prayer teaches. But men who do not worship, ultimately sacrifice one person to another. This is particularly true of those who seek to define men's energies and men's apocalypses in terms of what they do politically and socially for one another or against one another, be it in this generation or the next or the one after that. They ultimately forget that the relation of man to God is a reality in every generation, a reality that limits and defines precisely what we can and must do for one another in any generation.

The Trinity sufficient for salvation

The chief error of our time is, perhaps, the one that says that we shall be happy — happy by our labours and our means, happy because it is due to us, our "right", happy because we shall root out all the evil in our systems, if not in our hearts. But we shall not be so happy, and they who tell us otherwise must be firmly reminded that they but delude us. "Human beings", C.S. Lewis wrote, "can't make one another really happy for long".[8] And what was it Belloc said? "Whatever is buried right into our blood from immemorial habit that we must be certain to do if we are to be fairly happy (of course, no grown man or woman can really be very happy for long — but I mean reasonably happy . . .)".[7] The difference between being *happy* in this life and "reasonably happy" is fundamental. Which of the two we expect of this world probably defines as much about us as any other single criterion. If we worship at all, we must soon know that the two are not the same, that when we have by the grace of God achieved the second we are not by the same grace arrived at the first.

The recent Russian film of the Icons of André Rublēv has received much attention. Several years ago, Alexander Vetelev wrote beautifully of the meaning of the Trinity in these icons. He concluded:

> The communion of holy souls with God will be a communion of infinitely reciprocal love and the Trinity will be for them a super-loving unity. The mystery of the Holy Trinity, that mystery of the ineffable divine love, will be manifested to men only in the "future" age, in the Kingdom of the glory of God. Up to that moment, the mystery of the Holy Trinity is only given to us in "an enigma", only to the measure of the spiritual stature of grace and perfection in each one. But that much of the Holy Trinity which is communicated to us in Scripture, in the Church, in its liturgical, pastoral and iconographic experience, is fully sufficient for our salvation.

This sense of appreciation for our lot, for the fact that we have only a beginning, that what is promised in worship is so much more than what we actually will know, is the vital response of a human person to God, the trinitarian Source of our ultimate lives.

The relationship between worship, friendship and the Trinity is, of course, a close one.[11] The quality of worship, indeed, is not unconnected with how we believe in the triune God. In *Exodus*, we were told to have no other gods except Yahweh (20:3). Jesus told the woman at the well that "the hour will come — in fact, it is here already — when true worshippers will worship the Father in spirit and in truth: that is the kind of worship the Father wants" (Jn 4:23). Worship is sometimes spoken of as a "debt" we owe to God — and this is not wrong. When we worship in spirit and in truth we are, in a sense, exempt from place and condition. Each person is known by the Father. We must stand to our neighbour with the deepest realization of this, that what makes him what he is lies beyond us, that our neighbour too, even the one who chooses evil, reaches to God. And this is why we too as free are able to love our neighbour eternally, why he can, as can we, choose to reject his brother. Our true friendships will only touch a few of the billions of human beings who have lived on this planet. And this is enough and we can be content with it. It is our hatred, I suspect, that make us universal, make us ignore the complexity and particularity and uniqueness of each human person whom God has given to the world.

The lack of worship and contemplation, our sense that men are "nothing but creatures", is a dangerous one, since men who see nothing transcendent — for good or evil — reduce other people to the level of individual integers, who can be used or sacrificed for some cause judged to be more important. But Christianity in its belief in creation and resurrection teaches that there is no human "cause" or good that transcends the person. Worship is our conscious response to God — and it is this that lets us know our brother is of more significance than the universe, that incredible doctrine that lies at the heart of all biblical belief. Without vision, without worship, the people perish. If our era means anything, it means that this is quite literally true.

NOTES

¹ N. Gogol, *Meditations sur la Divine Liturgie.*
² *No Man Is an Island,* New York, Dell, 1963, pp. 235-37. Cf. also J.V. Schall, "The Totality of Society: From Justice to Friendship", *The Thomist,* January, 1957.
³ Jacques Maritain, "Marriage and Happiness", *Reflections on America,* New York, Scribner's, 1958, p. 140.
⁴ Schmemann, "Solzhenitsyn", *Russia Cristiana,* ¶129, Maggio-Giugno, 1973, pp. 47-48.
⁵ L. Kolakowski, "La diable peut-il être sauvé?" *Contrepoint,* ¶20, 1976, p. 138.
⁶ H. Belloc, *The Path to Rome,* Doubleday Image, 1956, pp. 38-39.
⁷ R. Voillaume, "La contemplazione nella Chiesa e nel mondo contemporaneo", *Contemplazione,* Assisi, *Cittadella,* 1970, pp. 27-28.
⁸ C.S. Lewis, *The Great Divorce,* London, Collins, 1946, p. 84.
⁹ Belloc, p. 39.
¹⁰ A. Vetelev, "La Teologia della 'Trinità' di Rublëv", *Russia Cristiana,* ¶137, Settembre-Ottobre, 1974, pp. 56-57.
¹¹ Cf. J.V. Schall, *Redeeming the Time,* New York, Sheed, 1968, Chapter 3.

Chapter XIV

ON GOD'S JOKES, TOYS, AND CHRISTMAS TREES

We men and women are, as I said before, "bad jokes" but funny still, supernatural creatures strayed into a natural world in which we really are not at home. We are persons. We worship. We pray. We laugh. We hate. We are lonely and are not silent enough. We are often bored even by beauty and grandeur. We are animals of a sort and live among the great beasts and tiny insects, which bite us sometimes 'and fascinate us. Yet we are transfused by our own doom and our destiny. The evil that exists among us, we choose too. And we have been told that we have been made for glory. There is nothing in the world that can contain what we are.

Here below, to speak that way, Joy is not the normal thing. But for this we were created. And if we cease to worship we cease to be who we are in our independence and our depth. We are indeed very fallen and quite fallible in all we do. Nonetheless, our Scriptures make so bold as to tell us that we were first loved. We are beyond use, useless in fact. We play and make the toys to which Plato once compared us, because he did not want to think we were created because God "had" to fashion us. We are the result of what did not need to be. And therefore we are full of surprise and drama — and, yes, risk too.

"Are 'educational' toys really educational?" Such was

a question once posed in a promotional advertisement for the *Saturday Review*. But as I thought about, I decided it was the wrong question. What should be asked rather was this: "Are 'educational' toys really *toys?*" This is the more profound inquiry, the one which most quickly brings us to the heart of those joyous and penetrating notions that are the very ground of our hope and our affection.

For it is the concept of a toy, of a thing made merely to be fascinating, that comes closest to touching the mystery of our strange worldly existence. Toys are not made for the purpose of education. Rather it is nearer to the truth to say that education is for the purpose of enabling us to play with toys — though, thank goodness, this capacity needs little education. Education is ever but a means, a preparation to arrive at something else, truth or technique. The question about toys already transcends the learning process. Indeed there is something mystical about a toy, something that touches the very spirit of the divine.

The God who does not exist

Neither George Bernard Shaw nor Count Leo Tolstoy was known as an adept theologizer. This did not, happily, prevent either from trying. We have a letter, belatedly published, from Shaw to Tolstoy.[1] Tolstoy, it appears, had chided Shaw for being too flippant about solemn things in *Man and Superman*. "But why should I not?" Shaw replied with gusto. "Why should humour and laughter be excommunicated? Suppose the world were *only one of God's jokes*, would you work any less to make it a good joke instead of a bad one?" In itself, this is a marvellous notion, as I have suggested — that the world is God's joke. The concept of joke, like that of toy, arises out of the exuberance of things, out of, it seems, the very source from which all things appear.

I should like to be more enthusiastic about Shaw's witty retort than I really am. Unfortunately, it immediately followed a brief exposition of the good man's theory of the deity, a quaint exposition, alas, that rather undermined any possibility of the world being a joke, good or bad.

To me God does not yet exist; but there is a creative force constantly struggling to evolve an executive organ of godlike knowledge and power: that is, to achieve omnipotence and omniscience; and every man and woman born is a fresh attempt to achieve this object.

The current belief that God already exists in perfection involves the belief that God deliberately created something lower than himself when he might just as easily have created something equally perfect. This is a horrible belief . . .

Such, of course, is refried Hegelianism, which ends up inventing what had just been denied. The suggestion that a perfect God create a plethora of equally Olympian divinities is rather contradictory. In bypassing the trinitarian mystery, moreover, Shaw's notion missed the very essence of diversity within the godhead as well as the profound dignity of creatures other than God. After all, because we are *not* God's equals, we do have a possibility to rejoice. Moreover, the belief that God will perhaps exist someday is merely despair for those who already do exist, just another version of sacrificing one person or generation to another. For Shaw we are more obviously tools than toys and jokes.

Credo in unum Deum, patrem omnipotentem . . . *Credo* in a creative force constantly struggling to evolve an executive organ of godlike knowledge and power . . . Which indeed is the more horrible belief? And how do we know that this "executive organ", once brought forth, will be benevolent? Shaw blithely presupposed, without telling us, the existence of a good God or at least a good process, to eliminate this fear.

M

Nevertheless, the notion that the world is one of God's jokes is, I think, a happy one. In Shaw's theology, everyone is supposed to become a kind of equal god some fine day, or at least somebody else is. In his humour, however, there seems to be some room for finiteness. A bad joke, after all, can often be as funny as a good one, as my friend who loved the bad jokes hinted. Out of a reflection on this notion of our finiteness and our jokes, I feel we can begin to conclude all of these reflections, as we grasp the essential glory of the fact that we are, none of us, nor the world itself, equally perfect to the deity. For the insistence that a perfect God is somehow imperfect because he does not create other "equally perfect gods" is simply a disbelief in and negation of the creature that does *not* have to be divine to be worthwhile, the creature we foolishly often call foolish, even worse, namely, ourselves. Sometimes, I believe, it takes far greater grace and faith to believe in the existence of ourselves than in the existence of God or a multitude thereof.

Marvin Glass is a toy designer who lived in Chicago. *The Wall Street Journal* once did a piece on his business and his attitudes.[2] Mr. Glass said that a good toy should have these qualities: "Several children should be able to play with it at once; it should also be easy to handle, not too complicated and preferably red". I cannot but wonder if that explains the colour of Santa Claus's uniform.

Mr. Glass told the Chicago City Council: "Only God can make a safe toy". Mr. Glass also believed, probably correctly, that there is a concerted plot on the part of broadcasters and other similar public-safety types to abolish imagination, to restrict severely the advertising of fantasy on children's programmes. The National Association of Broadcasters defined fantasy as "Anything not in the play environment or real world of children". I am glad C. S. Lewis never lived to hear such rot. "That is one of the functions of art", he wrote in his wonderful essay "On Stories", "to present what the narrow and desperately practical perspectives of real life exclude".[3]

Practically all the things that are worthwhile are not in the play environment or real world of children, except, of course, the children themselves — and they are always imagining. Mr. Glass went on: "When you deal with a toy, you deal with imagination. But if 'Jack and the Beanstalk' were written today, the author would have been told not to do it because vines can't grow that high and giants don't exist".

"Only God can make a safe toy . . ." I wonder if Mr. Glass knew that the ageing Plato, as I have mentioned before, in his *Laws*, called men the playthings of God? I hope he didn't, in a way. For these curious human toys that God did make are anything but "safe". That is, in fact, why God made them. For had the deity made men "safe", creátures with no real sense of doom, there would have been no sense in making men in the first place. *Because we are not safe, we are.*

The joy of getting

The trouble is that too many grim thinkers (not children) would assume Plato to have been merely frivolous for such a remark that men were the playthings, the toys, of God. But Plato was saying perhaps the most profound thing ever said before the *Prologue* of John, which said that the Word was made flesh and dwelt amongst us, a miracle of sorts making this world, after all, a dear and welcome place. Plato knew that the playthings of God are not safe, that they need not even exist, that they are, therefore, the results of creative joy.

In preparing for Christmas one year, Charlie Brown's little sister Sally was painfully writing her English theme. The subject was, "The True Meaning of Christmas". "To me", she painstakingly scribbled with her brother looking over her shoulder intently, "Christmas is the joy of getting". "Giving!" Charlie corrected her. But Sally refused to change her mind.

There is a profound insight here not unconnected with toys and Incarnation — the joy is in the getting. The degree to which this sounds merely selfish is the degree to which we have gotten away from the essence of our condition and our faith. To lack the capacity to enjoy the "getting" is to lack, perhaps, the best thing about us, the fact that what we have, we have received.

To be sure, we are likewise made to give, to go out. Malcolm Muggeridge, that sane man, not so long ago published his memoirs with the wonderful title, *Chronicles of Wasted Time*. (The Little Prince had said, hadn't he, that only the time you waste on your flower or on your star or on your friend is of any value?) "All I can claim to have learnt from the years I have spent in this world", Mr. Muggeridge wrote, "is that the only happiness is love, which is attained by giving, not receiving; and that the world itself only becomes the dear and habitable dwelling place it is when we who inhabit it know we are migrants, due when the time comes to fly away to other more commodious skies".

This is very Augustinian, very wise. And it is not untrue. "The joy of loving, of giving", a friend similarly wrote, "surely we are most truly blessed when we have a fellow creature to love, not to be loved *by*. Masses of people could love us and it wouldn't make a whit of difference. To have someone to love is to have a creature in whom reside the reasons for all the joy and pain and sorrow, ecstasy, concern and laughter of which we are capable, provided we are capable of giving at all". Our condition as persons in Christian tradition is also one of giving, no doubt. We are truly blessed by our love of our fellow creatures in giving. But it would be a strange world indeed if the only joy were in giving and not likewise in receiving, a very one-sided enthusiasm that takes the heart out of thanksgiving and gift and expectation. Our very capacity to love is already a gift that is not ours. This is the real meaning of toys, gifts and probably Christmas too.

Eric Mascall wrote in *Grace and Glory:*

> We love God, but only because God first loved us. The fact that God loved us provides us with both the reason for loving God and the power which enables us to do this. For the love which the Christian exercises whether towards God or towards men, is simply the reflection and overflow of the love which God has poured into him.[4]

When God did not make something equally perfect to himself, he indeed committed the "horror", as it were, of an unsafe toy and a bad joke. In the universe every man or woman is a fresh struggle in the search for omnipotence and omniscience. But the struggle takes place only under the more commodious skies of a reflection and an overflow enveloping us from the beginning. The joy is in the getting. We give only because we receive. When we cannot accept a gift, when we cannot be enthusiastic about receiving, the quality of our giving must also be suspect.

The First Coming and the Second

In *Eliot and His Age,* Russell Kirk mentioned a poem of Eliot entitled "The Cultivation of Christmas Trees", a poem found in the supplement to the English edition of The Liturgy of the Hours also. For Eliot, we are to remember the unexpectedness and wonder of our first glittering Christmas, of the goose and the turkey and the reverence and the gaiety, so that we shall retain to the end, in spite of it all, our sense of surprise and delight that such wondrous things could ever be at all — toys and jokes and gaiety and Christmas trees.

> Because the beginning shall remind us of the end
> And the first coming of the second coming.

We are not, blessed state, the equals of God. This is why we do in fact have creatures in whom reside the reasons for all the joy and pain and sorrow, ecstasy, concern and laughter of which we are capable. The joy is in the getting, in being the friends of such wonderful, unsafe toys and jokes whom God has made in lieu of making himself over and over again *ad infinitum.*

When we deal with a toy or a Christmas tree, we deal with imagination, with the capacity of wonder that suggests how our ordinary play world might be insufficient. Mr. Glass was right. There are men about today who would prevent our children from hearing the story of Jack and the Beanstalk for the first time, just as there are more and more men preventing our children from hearing the story of Christmas trees. Indeed, there are men who want, as the hope for mankind, to prevent children. But C.S. Lewis said, "Nature has that in her which compels us to invent giants". At the heart of every fairy tale is the human child astonished at the fears and glories and risks of the universe.

The child wonders at the Christmas tree:
Let him continue in the spirit of wonder
At the Feast as an event not accepted as a pretext. . .

The joy is in the getting — this is the event of the God who does yet exist.

The only happiness, then, is not "in love attained by giving, not receiving". That is a happiness, to be sure, and we should not doubt it. But the greater mystery is that someone loves us and gives us wondrous things — the End and the Beginning, the First Coming and the Second Coming. The joy in these is, and will be, in the getting. We are not gods. This is our glory and our wonder and the reason why we have other creatures whom we can love. With God's jokes, unsafe toys and glittering Christmas trees, with such is our universe filled.

The joy, dear friends, is in the getting.

NOTES

[1] Letter of 14 February 1910, in *The Intellectual Digest*, January, 1973, p. 32.
[2] December 1, 1972.
[3] *Of Other Worlds*, p. 10.
[4] p. 11.

Conclusion

ON LEADING OUR LIVES CALMLY AND CHEERFULLY

The worship of God by fallen men, men who are social animals and "sons of bitches", as God, the prophets and Arthur Miller have suggested, not without affection, seems to me now complete. I have stated my Odd Creed that Christianity needs nothing more than a refocusing on the First Great Commandment, a "need" that is at the same time "beyond need", a freedom, the ultimate one. Prayer and worship are, as Jacques Ellul intimated, the really revolutionary acts, the only ones that free us even from "the Revolution". That we men and women exist at all is, no doubt, "a risk". What else can the Creation accounts in *Genesis* mean but this?

God was dealt a pretty bad hand in our cosmic creation-game. I tried to suggest this when reflecting on play. Yet he has been playing it well, even when we insist on playing by our own rules, not his. Our human freedom is a risk that can reject the good, the order of salvation we have been given. We can even hate the kind of creatures we are in our very image, along with our moral laws that intimate we must choose even to remain, and rejoice in, the kind of men and women we are and can be.

Martin Luther in his treatise on Secular Authority remarked, " . . . It is always better to let a knave live than to kill a good man, for the world will still have knaves, and must have them, but of good men there are few". I have been concerned mostly, I suppose, with those of us who are mainly *knaves*. And there are more than just "knaves" in this world. I have not hesitated to include the depth of evil and hatred that exists too often among us. I am sure Christianity is right in insisting that we be not fooled by ideology and abstraction but firmly locate the origins of evil and pride and hatred in our hearts and our wills.

I found this poem during Lent, 1977:

> Ah world, I love you with all my heart . . .
> The sheep, the tree, the dog and the man
> are perfectly at peace. And my peace is at peace.
> Time and the earth lie down wonderfully together.
> The blacks probably do rape whites in jail,
> as Bill said in the coffee shop watching the game
> between Oakland and Cincinnati. And no doubt
> Karl was right that we should have volunteered
> as victims under the bombing of Hanoi.
> A guy said to Mishkin, "If you've seen all that,
> how can you go on saying you're happy?"[1]

But if there was slaughter in Hanoi there was slaughter in Hué too. My friend saw it. And these poem victims did not volunteer there either. Thus there is both apocalypse, the Lamb and the Lion lying down together, and the Doom which forbids us to be happy or to sing in the mountains because "We've seen all that".

Yet in this life we are only to expect a "reasonable happiness", as Belloc said. When we expect more, we verge on madness. The Cross is also a part of the faith. And there is no joy in Christendom without that Resurrection that redeems "all of that", that tells us that "God so loved the world . . . ". We can say, then, that we are happy, for we sometimes are. Our destiny does transcend what we do to one another. It is not ours to redeem ourselves. On being born human persons, we already reach the Godhead and its invitation to share its life, should we so choose, in the concrete limits of our own history, whatever it be.

If, then, there are knaves and tyrants, there are also good men and women, saints even, like Teresa, who told us, *God alone sufficeth*. If we are at all perceptive in our loves and in our hates, we must know that nothing else does suffice. So there are saints about, good men, kindly women. I am sure of this. I have met not a few. Yet I agree that our faith should not be only for the élite. The revelation of God was also, even mainly, meant for the rest of us ordinary folk — "knaves", "bad jokes", "son of bitches", "social animals", whatever we choose to call that very Christian truth that we are all weak and sinful and fallible, even on our way to *Glory*.

Nevertheless, this is what I mainly wanted to insist upon. We are in fact mainly men and women in search of glory. We are that very creature in the universe who can build something unnecessary and make it beautiful. We can do this because it has first been done to us. We need praise and beauty more than we do bread, even though we need bread too. "Our daily bread" is also one of our glories, and we should enjoy it. There is, as Lord Chesterfield recalled to us wisely, "No living in this world without a complaisant indulgence for other people's weaknesses".

Thus I am, with *Punch*, indeed prepared "To find a little bad in the best of things". And I have often laughed with tears in my eyes, often at my own foolishness, not a few times at the beauty I have unexpectedly discovered surprisingly before me. And I have wanted the world to have been made otherwise at times. I have wanted some other rules that would allow me what I wanted. But strangely, the Law and the Prophets always seemed to come up with better ways whenever I thought it all through, ways that better preserved what I wanted anyhow. My world was always too narrow. And hatred does exist, even hatred for the good, as the Gospels insist. So we should not be naïve, or not too much so.

Consequently in my walks and talks I have come to realize that "Things happen in life so fantastic that no imagination could have invented them". And it is this that brings us out onto the "Fields of Praise". We can go on saying we are happy, reasonably so, because our enemies can be loved. And we can be forgiven. There is a depth to us which no one but God fathoms. This is our final liberty from all the world which cannot comprehend us. So we are friends, but migrants too, on our way to "more commodious skies".

In *Utopia*, Thomas More wrote:

We have been ordained by God to this end: To follow nature is to conform to the dictates of reason on what we seek and avoid.

The first dictate of reason is ardently to love and revere the divine majesty, to whom we owe what we are and whatever happiness we can reach.

Secondly, reason warns us and summons us *to lead our lives as calmly and as cheerfully as we can,* and to help all others in nature's fellowship to attain this good.

I like that — the loving the divine majesty to whom we owe "whatever happiness", the leading our lives calmly and cheerfully.

We should not suppose that men cannot live Christian lives by suffering tyrannies, for that is the sad lot of so many even in our time. Nor should we think that we can achieve a paradise on earth, as so many of our ideologies now promise, quite *unreasonably,* as Thomas More would have said, on watching his own intellectual progeny in our time building their various utopias. Each person can be saved when and where he finds himself. Of the ultimate good, of that non-solitary life of the Trinity, we only get glimpses in our laughter and our joy. Sometimes we catch them too even in our sadness, on realizing that our city here in this world, our lovely city, with its Rathaus and its factory and its shops and its apartments, its Cathedral, University and Abbey church is, too, passing away.

Who are we? Why do we fail? What saves us? What are we to do when all else is done? — it seems remarkable to me that we must stick fairly close to the very ancient faith to see our way through the alternatives, through that "busy wickedness", from which Belloc told us to escape for a moment at morning Mass. But C. S. Lewis was right. *Joy is the serious business of heaven*. We are not fully at home here, even though in our humour, we suspect that joy might ultimately be so. We suspect that the Reverend Sumpter will, in the end, do little better at our own final eulogy than he did to W. C. Fields' friend, Ernest O. Potts. Each of us is fallible and finite, with more of the "rip" and the "knave" than we care to hear recounted.

But I have mainly wanted to call attention again to God, to his worship and all that surrounds it. This is what we have neglected to our peril, to our peril of being less than we already are. I have wondered whether we have any idea of the places, the depths, the beauty that comes to human life because such troublesome, humorous persons have praised the Lord.

Blessing and honour, glory and power, be unto him that sitteth on the throne, and unto the Lamb, forever, Amen.

The Alpha and the Omega. The First and the Last. The First Coming and the Second Coming.

In the beginning was the Word, and the Word was with God. And this Word became flesh and dwelt amongst us. From which we receive grace upon grace. No one knows the Father except the Son and him to whom the Son reveals him.

The joy, dear friends, is in the getting.

Indeed, it is "a damned strange world".

The worship of us fallen men, as calmly and as cheerfully as we can, shall go on precisely into everlasting.

And this too is what I oddly believe.

To conclude, finally, let me once more recall Meister Eckhart, "Nothing in all creation is so like God as stillness".

Listen . . . Ye "Knaves", "Bad Jokes", "Sons of Bitches", Fallen Men called to *Glory*, all companions of a Planet and a Past.

Listen . . . and Ye shall hear.

NOTE

[1] Linda Gregg, "The Beckett Kit", *The New Yorker*, 5 May 1975..